CW00649792

GILLES VILLENEUVE

By NIGEL ROEBUCK

HAZLETON PUBLISHING

PUBLISHER
Richard Poulter

EXECUTIVE PUBLISHER
Elizabeth Le Breton

ART EDITOR
Steve Small

PRODUCTION MANAGER
George Greenfield

PRODUCTION CONTROLLER
Peter Lovering

PRODUCTION ASSISTANT
Deirdre Fenney

STATISTICS
John Taylor

The colour photographs appearing on the front and back covers and pages 65-80 are by David Phipps.

Black and white photographs contributed by:
David Phipps, Nigel Snowdon, Diana Burnett, David Hutson, International Press Agency, Jeff Fisher, Marc Sproule, John Overton, Champion, Charles Knight and Marlboro.

This first edition published in 1990 by
Hazleton Publishing, 3 Richmond Hill, Richmond,
Surrey TW10 6RE.

ISBN: 0-905138-70-8

Printed in England by BAS Printers Ltd, Over Wallop, Hampshire.

Typesetting by First Impression Graphics Ltd, Richmond, Surrey.

DISTRIBUTORS

UK & OTHER MARKETS
Osprey Publishing Limited, 59 Grosvenor Street
London W1X 9DA

NORTH AMERICA
Motorbooks International, PO Box 2
729 Prospect Avenue, Osceola
Wisconsin 54020, USA

Paul Oxman Publishing, 17165 Newhope
Unit M, Fountain Valley, CA 92708, USA

AUSTRALIA
Technical Book & Magazine Co. Pty
289-299 Swanston Street
Melbourne, Victoria 3000

Universal Motor Publications
c/o Automoto Motoring Bookshop
152-154 Clarence Street
Sydney 2000, New South Wales

NEW ZEALAND
David Bateman Limited, PO Box 65062
Mairangi Bay, Auckland 10

SMEG
Gilles
LONGINES
27
MAGNETI MARELLI
personal
SCHMITTHELM
CHAMPION

GOODYEAR
Belgian Auto Club
PIRELLI
DATSUN
Nikon
Ford
DENIM
28
27
GOOD YEAR
27

LEVIOR
FLANG VAN LIMBURG

PROLOGUE

During the lunch break at Zolder that murky day, I wasted too much time in fruitless argument with Teddy Mayer of McLaren. Formula 1 was in a state of anarchy at the time, every paddock disfigured by acrimony, friendships splintered apart. On the aeroplane to Brussels I found myself next to a man I had known, and liked, a long time. Throughout the flight he stared out of the window, wordless and resolute.

A couple of weeks before, we had suffered FOCA's petulant boycott of the San Marino Grand Prix. I hadn't been in sympathy, and had written as much. Clearly, views at variance were not to be tolerated.

Mr Mayer and I found little common ground as we discussed the causes of the ferment, and at one point he – a lawyer! – accused me of having been 'bought' by Renault; only that, he suggested, could account for my aversion to what FOCA had done. By one o'clock, when the final session began, I was in a rage.

Others in the paddock were in a similar frame of mind. Ferrari had troubles of its own, internal troubles, over and above those assailing the sport in general. At Imola an unsuspecting Gilles Villeneuve had been robbed of certain and deserved victory when his team-mate, Didier Pironi, sprinted by him on the final lap. There was no time left for Gilles to respond. After the race he declared he would not speak to Pironi again, and here at Zolder he had held to his word.

For all that, he seemed calm enough as he sat in the Ferrari, preparing for one last qualifying lap on a used set of tyres. 'GV very composed,' I noted in my book – unaccountably, for GV was invariably composed as he prepared for a *banzai* lap. Then, with about ten minutes of the session remaining, he lifted his left arm, as he had done a thousand times and more; in went the electric starter, and the turbocharged V6 came alive.

As Villeneuve drove out, I wandered down the pit lane, chatting here and there. A couple of minutes or so later there was sudden silence, indicating the session was being stopped, but this happens so regularly as to occasion no real alarm: usually a car has pulled off in a spot adjudged dangerous, and needs to be towed in, nothing more.

But then there was that man's dreadful voice over the PA. Shouting almost hysterically, in English, he said that practice had been stopped 'because of an enormous accident to one of the Ferraris'. At that moment the surviving red car drifted into the pit lane, engine shut down, and I'm afraid to say my heart sank when I saw it was number 28.

So we set off running towards the chicane, up the hill and on down towards Terlamenbocht, hoping all the while, yet somehow feeling instinctively the presence of death.

It was like an aeroplane accident. The top rail of a barrier was twisted where the Ferrari had hit, and there was a deep pit in the sandy run-off where it had landed, nose first, in the midst of its furious flight; shards of red paint were everywhere.

Down the road, haphazardly parked, were Mass's March and Warwick's Toleman, and close by was what remained of number 27. Gilles, it transpired, had been thrown out of the car and into the catch-fencing, but we didn't know that as we turned around and stumbled back to the paddock. How bad? people asked, and we could only say as bad as it could be. Within an hour they ran the eight remaining minutes of the qualifying session; and within an hour of that there were those sweet souls who wondered aloud who would get the Ferrari drive. Teddy Mayer's earlier tastelessness fell into perspective.

In the days before Zolder was finally pensioned off as a Grand Prix circuit, we used always to stay at a small hotel in Genk, and the proprietor came to know us well. It was he who told us, as we sat around in desultory quiet that night, that Villeneuve was dead. For all we knew of his injuries, of the hopelessness of his condition, still the raw fact of his death was a shock. I was one of a multitude whose feelings for motor racing shifted for ever that weekend in May 1982.

Zolder, 8 May 1982. Above left: *Villeneuve leaves the pits during the Saturday morning session.* Left: *The shattered remains of the Ferrari after the accident in the afternoon.*

It was in the Formula Atlantic races at Trois Rivières that Gilles came to the notice of Formula 1 people. Top: *The Skiroule March (69) follows Jarier's Chevron (2) on the pace lap in 1975. By the time of the '77 race* (above) *Villeneuve knew his F1 future was assured.*

The name 'Villeneuve' began to register in Europe during the mid-Seventies. It was the fad then for a few Formula 1 stars to venture over to Quebec each autumn for the Formula Atlantic race through the streets of Trois Rivières. Patrick Depailler was one to make the trip in 1975, and he was suitably impressed: until his retirement, Gilles had been running ahead of him.

A year later, though, James Hunt came back raving about Villeneuve and, as a man on the point of becoming World Champion, his opinion had real bite. Hunt went to Trois Rivières to drive a March for Ecurie Canada, with Gilles and Depailler as his team-mates. Alan Jones and Patrick Tambay were also there. Villeneuve slayed them all, and in deft, crushing, style.

'You only needed to watch him for a couple of minutes to know,' James said. 'I mean, he was *quick*! We were driving identical cars for the same team, so I knew. OK, he was doing what he was used to, and I wasn't, but in Formula 1 I reckoned I was as quick as anyone at that time, and I couldn't get near him. He looked to me like a very special talent, and I told Marlboro and McLaren we needed him in the team as soon as possible.'

First Grand Prix: Silverstone 1977.

Hence, at Silverstone the following summer, there was the name of G. Villeneuve tucked away at the foot of the entry list in the British Grand Prix programme. Hunt and Jochen Mass were the regular McLaren drivers, both in M26 cars, and Gilles was assigned an older M23, number 40.

Before he arrived, I had heard all about him from Chris Amon, who had retired earlier that summer, handing over to Villeneuve the wheel of the awful Wolf Dallara Can-Am car.

'This guy', Amon said on the phone, 'is something else again. In 15 years of racing, I've never seen anyone behave like he does after a shunt – I mean, he doesn't react at all! It's just like nothing has happened, but the state of the car tells you different...'

'Is he quick?' I asked. Racing's universal question.

'Quick?' Chris for once raised his voice. 'He's quicker than anyone I've ever *seen*!'

His words were in my mind as I watched Gilles test the McLaren, which he did in unorthodox style: countless laps, countless spins. More than once, leaving his braking later and later, he stalled the engine going into a corner. But he never hit anything. And his times were remarkable.

He was very quiet and shy that first weekend, perhaps a little overawed by the power of a first World Championship Grand Prix, but assuredly drinking everything in. This was what he wanted, and he looked as though born to it. Whatever 'charisma' may be, we could see it was there, and to throw away. He shook hands firmly, smiled a lot, and gabbled in that curious and unfamiliar patois, like a Frenchman who had lived a long time in North America.

Hadn't he spun rather a lot? someone said, and Gilles grinned at the question. 'Yes,' he said. 'Of course. This is what I want to do – Formula 1. Originally, I was supposed to have several races with McLaren this year, but now it looks like this could be the only one. This is the fastest car I've ever driven, and the fastest track I've ever seen. I had to learn both in a short time, and the simplest way to find the limit is to go quicker and quicker until you go over it. Then you come back from that a bit, and think about the next corner.'

It was a novel approach, you had to say, but it seemed to work. In practice Villeneuve had his corners together well enough to qualify ninth, way quicker than Mass. In the early going he ran an easy seventh before pitting with what seemed to be overheating, but proved to be merely a faulty temperature gauge. Livid, he went back out to chase the remnants of his chance to impress, and set fifth-best lap, faster than such as Lauda and Andretti. Hunt, who won, had been right: this was indeed a talent.

On his Grand Prix debut Gilles amazed everyone with his speed and aggression in the McLaren M23, comfortably outpacing Jochen Mass, a regular member of the team.

Mosport Park 1977. Villeneuve's Ferrari debut did not go as he would have wished. On Goodyears, the T2 was a cranky car to drive and well off the pace. For all that, though, Gilles was already starting to enjoy Ferrari life, and driving in the style we came to take for granted.

We met again at Watkins Glen in the autumn, and by now Villeneuve's circumstances had changed. Another of Teddy Mayer's unfathomable decisions had led to the signing of Patrick Tambay, rather than Gilles, at McLaren. But Enzo Ferrari, casting away the habits of a lifetime, had taken a chance on a virtual unknown. He just had a feeling, he said, about this little fellow from Quebec.

At the Glen Gilles shivered away in a thick red lumber-jacket, reluctantly taking his hand from his pocket as well-wishers came up to offer congratulations on his new employment. He was there merely as a Ferrari guest, to watch Lauda and Reutemann, but by the next race, at Mosport Park, he was Carlos's team-mate. Niki, after scoring enough points at the Glen to lock up the championship, had scuttled back to Austria.

Beta
GOODYEAR
gilles villeneuve

GOODYEAR

Above right: *In Canada the furiously driven Ferrari finally retired with a broken driveshaft, leaving Villeneuve* (above) *to walk in.*

At Fuji (right) *the Ferrari, here leading Hoshino's Kojima, was almost undrivable, and Villeneuve eventually had a huge accident with Peterson's Tyrrell.*

Marlboro
Agip
HEUER
21

UNI-PEX
HEUER
11

In late 1977 the Ferrari T2 on Goodyears was a far from competitive proposition, and in his anxiety to shine before his own people Gilles spun more than once, finally breaking a driveshaft as he rejoined the circuit. At Fuji, his second race, he crashed catastrophically after tangling with Peterson's Tyrrell. The Ferrari somersaulted, and two spectators, standing in a prohibited area, were killed. In Europe word grew that Enzo might be having second thoughts about his new driver.

It was all hokum, of course. After more than half a century in motor racing, Ferrari did not throw out a driver on the strength of two accidents. Accordingly, Gilles moved his family to Europe, renting a villa at Plascassier, in the hills above Cannes. Then he settled to a winter of testing.

The new season, though, continued in the fashion of the old. In Buenos Aires there were several spins, and at Rio another accident involving Peterson. By now Ronnie was developing a persecution complex: 'Why me? Why does he always pick on me?' Gilles, for whom Peterson was a hero, said Ronnie had braked earlier than he had expected...

At Long Beach there was yet another shunt, this time over the top of Regazzoni's Shadow, which was being lapped. But into the minds of the sceptics were now coming thoughts that maybe this fellow was something special, after all: when Gilles hit Clay, he was leading, and had been since the start. It was but the sixth Grand Prix of his career.

Monaco: yes, an accident, but this time the consequence of tyre failure in the tunnel. I saw him within a few minutes, and was nonplussed by the complete absence of any sense of fright. Amon's remarks came back to me.

At Zolder I taped the first of many Villeneuve interviews. We sat in the Ferrari transporter, and I started by taking him back to the shunt in Monte Carlo. It had been, after all, what Jackie Stewart would call 'a fairly important accident'. Do you have no sense of imagination? I began. Or what?

'I don't have any fear of a crash,' Gilles replied. 'No fear of that. OK, on a fifth-gear corner I don't want to crash – I'm not crazy. If I feel I'm going to put a wheel on the grass, I'm going to lift a bit, like anyone else. But if it's near the end of qualifying, and you're trying for pole position maybe, then I guess you can squeeze the fear...'

In light of what happened in the same place four years later, those words chill now. Indeed, so many of Villeneuve's remarks fell into different perspective after his death. But at the time they were made calmly and with freshness; no matter how much bravado he may have brought to his work, there was none in his manner.

I persisted with the Monaco accident. Had he not been frightened at all?

'For me, no. For the car, yes. I thought, "Bloody hell, I'm going to have a nice one here!" But, you know, you just go like this...' And he broke off, screwing up his face, sticking his arms out in front of him, as if bracing himself for an impact.

'In that split-second, what came into my mind was that I wasn't going to finish the race, that two points were going away. That was the thought I had. I never think I can hurt myself, but I know I can hurt the car, and that's what I don't want to do.'

Villeneuve had no doubt that this apparent fearlessness had its roots in his snowmobile days. In 1974 he had won the World Championship, and people still shudder who saw him pitching the tiny machines over sundry frozen lakes in Quebec.

'Every winter you would reckon on three or four big spills,' he recalled, 'and that meant being thrown onto ice at maybe 100 mph. But I never hurt myself on a snowmobile – not seriously. And I think accidents always look worse to spectators than they feel to the driver.'

Already he was completely in love with life at Ferrari. As we talked that Saturday afternoon the mechanics were in exuberant mood, for Carlos Reutemann had qualified second, Gilles fourth. When things went well, they would sing, and now, further boosted by Lambrusco, they were giving forth with gusto. This was another time, when passion and spontaneity were still paramount at Maranello, when Ferrari was simply itself. The dour 'corporate' era was yet to come, and Villeneuve grinned as he cocked an ear to the boys' song.

This was 1978, the year of the Lotus 79. The following day Mario Andretti led the Belgian Grand Prix from beginning to end, but Gilles ran a comfortable second before – as at Monaco – puncturing a front tyre. Finally he finished fourth.

Through that summer we got to know each other well. Usually, conversations at race tracks between drivers and journalists are confined to the problems of the day; and, as such, are rarely stimulating or memorable. But at the time I was in the habit of writing stories about drivers from the past, and one day told Gilles he put me in mind of Nuvolari and Rosemeyer.

Most contemporary Grand Prix drivers, you find, have an interest in the sport which began the day they did, but Villeneuve was entranced with its history. 'Tell me about those guys,' he would say. OK, what do you want to know? '*Everything!*'

So we would sit and talk, and Joann would serve up her famous hamburgers. Even had I disliked Gilles on sight, the temptation would have been strong to get along with him, for I shared his horror of *nouvelle cuisine*, and quickly came to recognise the

Snowmobile days. Gilles was World Champion in 1974, and always reckoned his apparent fearlessness in cars was born here.

Marlboro
WORLD CHAMPIONSHIP TEAM
Marlboro
Matras
MICHELIN
12
MICHELIN

Left: *Ferrari had an on-off year in 1978, with the T3 and Michelin tyres. Pensive perhaps about the superiority of the Lotus 79, Gilles was nevertheless to win before the year was out.* Below left: *Villeneuve leads Depailler's Tyrrell at Paul Ricard.*

camper with the Quebec plates as the best restaurant in the place – whatever the place.

'I can't remember exactly when I got interested in racing,' he said one day, 'but I always loved speed. It's the earliest sensation I can recall. My father used to drive very fast, and from being six years old I can remember telling him to go quicker, to pass the guy in front. He got a lot of tickets because of me, I guess.

'At about that age, I used to sit on his knee and steer. So I just loved cars, but my first real touch with racing was a TransAm race at St Jovite, when I was about 17. They had Formula Fords there, as well, and I thought eighty per cent of the drivers were wankers – you know, guys with a lot of money, going very slowly. I'd been racing snowmobiles a while by then, but I knew that day this was what I wanted for my life.'

At times like this, when there was no particular hurry, Gilles relaxed the pace of his speech. Whenever he talked about his feelings for racing, it was with quiet and reflective emotion, almost as if speaking of the love of his life. Probably, he was.

Once I asked him what he might do when he had given up driving. From his expression, it had never crossed his mind.

'I don't want to think about it,' he replied, 'because I can't imagine life without it.'

There will surely come a time, though, I persisted; perhaps when you've won the World Championship more than once.... And it was now I came to realise how different he was from other drivers I had known.

'I don't *need* the championship,' he said. 'Not in the way someone like Pironi does. That's the only reason he's a racing driver: he must be World Champion. And that makes me sorry for him – what's he going to do when he's won it? I think probably he'll quit. For Didier, it's just like a mountain he has to climb, and he only has to do it once – just get there and stick in a flag with his name on it. I don't understand people like him, because they seem to need that to be sure how good they are. Then they're happy to leave it, and do something else.

'If I win the championship one day, OK, I'm not going to turn it away! But, you know, plenty of drivers have won it who were not so great – and yet a guy like Ronnie Peterson never won it. So how much is it worth? Can anyone really *feel* like a World Champion when he's only won two races or something – when he got beaten 14 times? No, to me being World Champion is not so important.

'What I care about', he went on, after a pause, 'is being the best. And it doesn't matter what other people think. You don't have to go and get some trophy from Balestre at the end of the season. You have to *know* you can drive a race car faster than anyone else. Maybe I'm wrong, but that's the feeling that I have, and that's why I'm a happy man.

When I don't have it any more, I'll stop. But so long as I do, all I want is to win races. And if my car won't let me, I can still have in my head the thought that no one could have driven it as fast as I did – even if I was only tenth. That's why I find it easy to drive hard all the time.'

All of that explained a lot about Gilles Villeneuve. For most of his four-and-a-bit years in Formula 1 he never had a car remotely comparable with the best. It was the time of the ground-effect era, when generally you were squarely as competitive as your skirts allowed you to be. Ferrari horsepower compensated a little, of course, but Maranello's adherence to the low and wide flat-12 engine militated against the building of a genuine ground-effect car.

In 1978, when Gilles was learning his craft, only the Lotus 79 had this seal with the ground which would become intrinsic to Formula 1. There was no answer to Andretti and Peterson, but Ferrari's T3 worried them most, and through the year the performance gap shrank between Reutemann and Villeneuve. By Monza it was Gilles, not Carlos, who joined Andretti on the front row; Gilles, too, who took the lead.

As he headed down towards the first chicane, there was devastation behind, an appalling and fiery multiple accident, which would ultimately cost the life of Ronnie Peterson. Nearly two hours passed as marshals laboured away to clear the wreckage; then the field set off on another formation lap, in the course of which Scheckter's Wolf broke a stub-axle at the second Lesmo, hitting the barrier hard enough almost to flatten it.

Out of their cars once more, the drivers were now completely distraught, some of them talking of going home at once. Whatever, they said, they would not start the race until the damaged guard rail had been replaced. In the stands, the volatile *tifosi* began to get restless. The entire scene was something from hell.

In the course of this further hour-long delay, Villeneuve alone remained in his car, helmet on, belts secured. 'I didn't want to get involved,' he said. 'Obviously, there was going to be a race eventually – otherwise there'd have been a riot. I looked at the drivers around me, saw their faces, and obviously they were getting more and more agitated. I didn't think that was a good frame of mind to be in at the start of a Grand Prix, so I deliberately stayed clear of it.'

When they got the signal to go, Gilles was more ready than anyone – too ready, in fact. The man on the start button, having earlier pressed it too soon, this time waited endlessly. His clutch creeping, Villeneuve finally went, and did not make the classic mistake of lifting off after getting away early. He kept his foot hard in it, and Andretti went with him.

Gilles led most of the way, but his Michelins began to go off, and Mario got him with a few laps to go. Afterwards, though, both were docked a minute for jumping the start, which put them back to sixth and seventh. It was a final act of farce with which to close one of racing's most dreadful days, but the Italians were confirmed in their belief that Villeneuve was the new messiah.

Andretti, too, was impressed that day: 'Gilles really had matured by that time. He drove to the limit of the car, and he made no mistakes. And I knew when I made an attempt to go by him he was going to give me some race track. He didn't give me the big old chop, which showed the kid was thinking...'

It would become a recurrent theme of Villeneuve's racing life. Sometimes other drivers would shake their heads at what they saw as a piece of craziness, but always they stressed his absolute fairness in a fight.

'To Gilles, racing truly was a *sport*,' says Keke Rosberg, 'which is why he would never chop you. Something like that he'd look on with contempt. You didn't have to be a good driver to do that, let alone a great one. *Anyone* could do that. Gilles was the hardest bastard I ever raced against, but completely fair. If you'd beaten him to a corner, he accepted it, and gave you room. Then he'd be right back at you at the next one! Sure, he took unbelievable risks – but only with himself. And that's why I get pissed off now when people compare Senna with him. Gilles was a giant of a driver, yes, but he was also a great man.'

After Monza, it was clear that Villeneuve's first Grand Prix victory was on the near horizon, and it came where he might have dreamed. Montreal hosted a World Championship race for the first time that autumn, and Gilles won. The day was freezing blue, and Prime Minister Pierre Trudeau was among those there to salute this new Canadian national hero. They did not see a flag-to-flag triumph for the number 12 Ferrari, most of the race being led by Jarier's Lotus, but when the Frenchman retired Gilles was on hand to benefit.

'I wish I could rerun that day,' he said, thinking back to it a couple of years later, 'because I have virtually no memory of it, and I didn't savour it as much as I should have done. Somehow, the aftermath of the race was all a bit too much, and I seemed to be in a dream. I'd always hoped I'd win my first race after *paralysing* them, I guess. OK, I drove flat out most of the way, and there was no chance of beating the Lotus round there, but the day was a little marred for me because I felt I'd inherited it.'

Not for Villeneuve the 'nine points are nine points' mentality. The theatre of motor racing was always important. Ask most drivers to describe their ideal race, and they

NTS INDY 500
Pièces et accessoires d'auto
Marlboro
Labatt
Agip
12
HEUER
Agip
MICHELIN

It was very important to Gilles that he showed well in Montreal, before his own people. In wet practice (above left) *he was naturally in his element, and on race day* (left) *he duly won, after Jarier's retirement.* Above: *First Grand Prix win – and at home. At the time it was almost too much to take in...*

CONNOISSEUR BRANDY

GOODYEAR
Simba

Kyalami 1979, and the debut of the Ferrari T4. Left: *Villeneuve* (left) *and Scheckter lead the pack away. Later it dried out, but the red cars remained untouchable. Jody graciously salutes Gilles on the rostrum* (below left)*, as third man Jarier looks on.*

will come out with 'one where I lead from start to finish' or even 'any one I win'. Gilles said, no, in his perfect race he would start from the pole, lead easily for a while, get a puncture, lose nearly a lap, then pass everyone again, taking the lead at the last corner of the last lap.

In terms of results, his great year was 1979, the year of the Ferrari T4. Like its predecessor, it was no kind of genuine ground-effect car, for that wide flat-12 remained the limiting factor. Conversely, the engine retained a power advantage over the Cosworth V8, and in a straight line was beaten only by Renault's turbocharged V6.

It was a deft car, the T4, its inherent lack of grip only truly noticeable through very fast corners. At Silverstone, for example, it was hopeless, left behind especially by the new Williams FW07. But usually Gilles and new team-mate Jody Scheckter were there or thereabouts.

In 1979 the Villeneuve legend took root. He played a central role in virtually every race of the year, and in the early part of the season looked a shoe-in for the World Championship. At Kyalami the T4 made its debut, and Gilles and Jody finished 1–2; at Long Beach they did the same. For the Brands Hatch Race of Champions Ferrari made a token entry, sending over a single T3. Result? Villeneuve, Piquet, Andretti.

At around that time I interviewed Jackie Stewart, asking him for his thoughts on the state of Formula 1. Did he see Gilles as the 1979 World Champion? Stewart, as always, was perceptive.

'I think Ferrari will be World Champions this year,' he said, 'and I think in the end it will be Scheckter. If you spoke to Gilles Villeneuve now, asked him to consider the tools he has to work with and the experience he has to manipulate those tools, I think he would admit he's not quite ready to be World Champion. Scheckter, on the other hand, is; he's not a dominant winner at this time, but he is a winner. Jody drives conservatively now, and he's maturing, which is not true of most top-line drivers today.'

And Gilles? 'Oh, I think he's superb, and I believe he'll get better and better. At the moment he still makes mistakes, misses the odd apex, gets up on a kerb, uses a little too much road on the way out sometimes, but I'm being hypercritical here. His level of natural talent is phenomenal – there's real genius in his car control.'

A worry in Stewart's mind at the time was that the politics indigenous to Maranello might ultimately disrupt the harmony between the two drivers. 'They're very good at sowing the seeds of suspicion in people's minds at Ferrari, which can disturb even a very strong friendship. Suspicion is something no man needs, especially in a sport as

It was easy for Villeneuve at Long Beach in '79. He started from the pole, and in the early laps (right) *led from Depailler and Scheckter.* Below right: *Reutemann's Lotus (2) looked like the main opposition, but was in trouble from the start.*

competitive as racing.'

In this case, his fears were groundless. Through the last days of his life, Villeneuve faced precisely that problem with Didier Pironi, but from the start he and Scheckter operated as partners, worked together with absolute trust. 'In all my time at Ferrari', Mauro Forghieri says, 'the years with Gilles and Jody were the happiest. Villeneuve... had a competitiveness which I have never seen in any other driver, a *rage* to win. People tell me Senna is the same now, but I wouldn't know. The amazing thing about Gilles was that he was only that way in a car; as soon as he was out of it, he was relaxed, laughing. He *loved* his life, Gilles, and I don't have the same impression of Senna. When Gilles drove, he drove with such joy, such pleasure...'

This was an aspect of Villeneuve's character that Scheckter found hard to understand. 'In our attitude to motor racing, we were absolute opposites,' Jody says. 'It was a romantic thing for him, whereas my absolute priority was keeping myself alive – I felt, you know, that the axe was always against my neck. But Gilles had to be quickest on *every* lap, even in a weekday test at Fiorano.

'I thought then – and I will always think – he was the fastest racing driver there has ever been, and I know there is nothing I could say which would please him more than that.

'For me, it seemed obvious the main reason for going motor racing was to win the World Championship, and I think that applies to almost everyone who gets in a Formula 1 car. But not Gilles. Winning races was everything to him, but he didn't care that much about titles. What was unique in him was that he never got disheartened by poor cars; if the thing was good for tenth place, OK, he'd drive his balls off to be ninth – and if he made it, he'd be as happy afterwards as if he'd won. For him, the important thing was to *know* his car could not have been driven faster. And, of course, he knew that every time he ever got out of a car.

'If he could come back and live his life again, I'm sure he would do exactly the same – and with the same love. That's the right word, too. Gilles was in love with motor racing.'

Jackie Stewart proved to be right about 1979. Villeneuve it was who laid on the passion, made the news, but Scheckter quietly racked up the points, capitalised on Ferrari reliability. And there were times when Jody was a genuine match for Gilles. At Monte Carlo, for example, he led all the way, and from pole position. But Zolder said most about the way of the year for the two men.

On the second lap Scheckter tangled with Clay Regazzoni at the chicane, and Villeneuve went clean over the Williams. Jody's car survived intact, but Gilles needed to

Overleaf: *Gilles made it three wins in three races by taking the Race of Champions in 1979, despite using an old T3. Andretti's Lotus 79 (1) led for much of the way, but Villeneuve chased him down at this, one of his favourite circuits. It was to be his only win in England.*

END
FREEWAY
Canon
JOHNSON LIFT
BELL
BELL
WINNEBAGO
Lubri
Lon
Lubri
Lon
MICHELIN MICHELIN
12
25
elf
KLOS 95½

JOHNSON LIFT
BELL
BELL
WINNEBAGO
KLOS 95½
MARTINI
TISSOT
2
Valvoline
Valvoline
MICHELIN MICHELIN
12
12
Agip

NI RACING
MARTINI
LOTUS
1
GOOD YEAR

Marlboro
Labatt
Agip
12
HEUER
MICHELIN

Marlboro
LONGINES
elf
MICHELIN MICHELIN
MICHELIN
Agip
FIAT
Gilles Villeneuve
12
Agip
speedline
SKF
arexons
brembo
12
Agip
MICHELIN

One of Villeneuve's greatest drives came at Zolder in 1979. Involved in someone else's accident soon after the start, he stopped at the pits, then drove from last to third – only to run out of fuel within sight of the flag.

stop for a new nose cone. When the Ferrari came back out, it was 23rd, and last.

At the front there was a scrap between Ligier (Jacques Laffite and Patrick Depailler) and Williams (Alan Jones), with Scheckter a lonesome fourth – which gradually became first, as the leaders fell. But no one took a lot of notice of Jody's afternoon; all the attention was on the other Ferrari, which was running as if on an endless succession of qualifying laps. With eight to go, Villeneuve was up in third, and closing on Laffite.

Gilles got to within 200 yards of the flag before the flat-12 coughed for the last time, and fell silent. So hard had been his charge that Ferrari's fuel calculations were thrown awry. He arrived at the pits on foot, four points gone. He would lose the championship to Scheckter by precisely that number.

Some of the early-season euphoria began to evaporate at Járama (left)*, where Villeneuve lost time with a couple of spins and a tyre change. Seventh place – and fastest lap – was his lot for the day.* Above left: *In his efforts to stay with Depailler's winning Ligier, Gilles used more road than the track designer had intended.*

All over Europe Villeneuve caused sensation that summer. His freestyle combat with René Arnoux's Renault in the closing laps at Dijon remains the supreme example of joyous and uninhibited *racing*.

It lasted only a few laps, a few minutes, but no one really knows how many times those two cars banged wheels, slid wide, went off the road. There was a desperate frenzy about it, yet also the feeling these two fellows were trying to take care of each other. No flicker of malice was apparent, and within yards of taking the flag – Villeneuve in front – the red car and the yellow were side by side, their drivers' hands raised in mutual salute. Back at the pits, they climbed out and embraced. It had been good and fair, and there was no need for recrimination.

'*Jesus*, that was fun!' Gilles exclaimed. 'I thought for sure we were going to get on our heads, you know, because when you start interlocking wheels it's very easy for one car to climb over the other...'

In November 1989, as Arnoux prepared for his last Grand Prix, I asked which had been the most memorable. René's was, after all, a considerable Formula 1 career, and you might have expected him to cite one of his victories for Renault or Ferrari, but no. 'Dijon '79,' he replied at once. 'The duel with Gilles is something I'll never forget, my greatest *souvenir* of racing. You can only race like that, you know, with someone you trust completely, and you don't meet many people like him. He beat me, yes, and in France, but it didn't worry me – I knew I'd been beaten by the best driver in the world.

'It was terrible when Gilles died,' Arnoux went on. 'I cried that day, and the next one, too, even though I had to race. And I remember the feeling that we were all starting equal, from now on. Villeneuve was gone. We all knew he had a talent beyond our reach.'

For all their respect for his ability, however, some of Gilles's senior fellows shook disapproving heads at Dijon, and before the British Grand Prix they sought to carpet him and Arnoux. Neither man was much impressed. 'We were risking only ourselves,' Villeneuve muttered at Silverstone, 'and they missed the point completely – which was that René and I had a clean fight. OK, it was dangerous – motor racing *is* dangerous! But neither of us did anything dirty. I guess they would have liked it more if I'd just given up. But I ask you, what does "racing driver" mean? To me, it's a driver who *races*...'

Predictably, Mario Andretti was one member of the old guard who concurred. 'What's the problem?' he drawled. 'This was just a coupla young lions clawin' each other – why are these guys so upset?' Gilles liked that.

Arnoux and Villeneuve, pictured here in 1981, fought at the '79 French Grand Prix a battle which has gone into motor racing legend.

At Dijon it was Villeneuve against the Renaults, with no one else close. Jabouille eventually powered by the Ferrari into the lead, but Gilles – tyres finished – somehow resisted Arnoux.

The Gitanes lady's gesture (above right) *is exactly right. Villeneuve and Arnoux take the flag at Dijon.* Right: *Jabouille celebrates his win, Arnoux looks bemused, and Villeneuve's face reflects the intensity of those final laps.*

EVIAN
CASINO ROYAL
GITANES
CIRCUIT PAUL RICARD
GLACES GERVAIS

Monte Carlo
MOET
Labatt
Marlboro
MICHELIN
CHAMPION
elf
R.M.O

Above right: *At Silverstone the Ferrari T4's inherent lack of downforce made itself felt, neither Villeneuve nor Scheckter ever figuring seriously. Gilles made a fantastic start at Zeltweg* (right), *leading Jones's Williams for a while. Eventually, though, he had to settle for second.*

ritish Grand Prix
DAILY EXPRESS
12
Mobil
Mobil
Hella-Licht S

MICHELIN MICHELIN
Marlboro
Agip
12
12
HEUER
Agip
MICHELIN
Agip

The Dutch Grand Prix was Villeneuve in extremis. *He passed Jones's faster Williams for the lead, and stayed there until a rear tyre began to go down.*

More censure came his way, however, in the aftermath of Zandvoort, where we had Villeneuve *in extremis*. By now the Williams FW07 was as reliable as it was fleet, and Alan Jones was on a roll. Always, though, it was Villeneuve's T4 which constituted the major threat: 'It got to the point when I started to believe the mechanics had painted the bloody mirrors red.'

In Holland Alan led the opening laps, but Gilles somehow passed him on the outside of the right-handed Tarzan, and stayed ahead to within 30 laps of the finish, at which point his left-rear tyre developed a slow puncture, causing a spin. His freakish proprioception worked for him here, the Ferrari continuing on its way without ever coming to rest. But a lap later the failing Michelin blew apart on the pit straight, and again Villeneuve was into a lurid spin, finishing up on the grass, his race apparently done.

Instead of abandoning the car, though, Gilles stayed put, pushing up his visor and stabbing at the starter button. For several seconds the flat-12 churned away, then finally caught, and we looked on in amazement as the car went on its three-wheeled way at what seemed an extravagant rate. By the time it reached the pits, the entire left-rear corner was trailing.

Some members of the 'knitting circle' were barely able to control their indignation, and before Monza Villeneuve was given a lecture. In Italy he defended his actions.

'Having seen the TV coverage, I can understand some of the criticism,' he allowed. 'There was no problem in coming back on three wheels, but when the wheel was hanging behind, OK, I accept it could have caused a big accident for someone else, and I regret that. But I had no idea it was there – I thought it had gone! I couldn't see it in my mirrors. So I'm sorry for that.

'On the other hand...' He wasn't finished. 'On the other hand, I've no regrets about trying to get back to the pits in the first place. As long as the car will run, I will try and get it to the pits, and I think if you don't do that you are not a racing driver. After the spin the car was in a very dangerous place, and it would have been stupid to leave it there, because the marshals couldn't have moved it. So I set off, and the car was very easy to drive on three wheels. Really. I only used third gear, but I could have used fifth...

'I will always accept criticism if it's justified,' Gilles concluded, 'but the Zandvoort thing – however bad it looked on TV – was different. My conscience is clear. And honestly I don't care what people are saying about that; I won't change my driving for them.'

MICHELIN
Agip
FIAT
MAGNETI MARELLI
Agip
CHAMPION
brembo
arexons
SKF
speedline
12

Zandvoort 1979. Left: *The Ferrari comes to rest before Tarzan, left-rear tyre shredded. Gilles restarts the engine* (below left), *and prepares to set off. Echoing Nuvolari, he three-wheels his way back to the pits* (below), *but there wasn't a whole lot the mechanics could do…*

Marlboro
12
MICHELIN

At Monza (left) *Gilles dutifully followed Scheckter throughout – knowing he had only to pass to become World Champion.* Below left: *The two friends celebrated together on the rostrum.*

There could be no cause for complaint in the Italian Grand Prix, where Villeneuve dutifully tailed Scheckter all the way. To sit behind your team-mate, knowing you have only to pass him to win the World Championship, puts high call on a driver's integrity, but no one ever doubted that in Gilles. The two T4s crossed the line a few yards apart. On the rostrum both men smiled.

Could he have passed Jody that day? Gilles was always evasive about that: 'Of course I *believe* I could, sure. But I knew the rules of the game, and I'd given my word.'

Was he not even tempted to run at the front for a few laps? 'Not really. It would have been false, wouldn't it? And not a particularly nice thing to do, either, because this was Jody's day. I didn't need to go through that whole thing of showing the crowd I was quicker, and just being a good boy. No, I would never have tried to pass him. Mind you,' he concluded, 'I sat there, staring at his engine all afternoon, and hoping like hell it would blow!'

It didn't. Monza confirmed Scheckter as the 1979 World Champion, and now Villeneuve happily contemplated the last two races of the season, at Montreal and Watkins Glen. With the title decided, team orders were done for the year: he could simply go for it.

Both the North American Grands Prix were magnificent races, each coming down to a straight fight between Gilles and Alan Jones. In Canada Villeneuve led from the start, holding off the indubitably faster Williams for 50 of the 72 laps, the rest bit-players for the day. But then Alan took a run down the inside of the Ferrari into the hairpin, and bundled his way through. It was hard but fair, precisely the kind of driving Gilles practised himself.

'I thought, "I've done it!"' Jones remembered, 'and once I was into the lead I built up a bit of a cushion. But as soon as I backed off a fraction, there was that bloody red shitbox in my mirrors again! Villeneuve was unbelievable like that – I mean, he *never* gave up. He was the best driver I ever raced against, I think, and I certainly enjoyed my fights with him more than with anyone else, because I always knew exactly where I was with him. He'd never drive straight at you or edge you into a wall, or any of that stuff.

'...as soon as I backed off a fraction, there was that bloody red shitbox in my mirrors again!' Jones just holds off Villeneuve to the flag, at Montreal in 1979.

At Watkins Glen (right) *it was Villeneuve versus Jones again, the Ferrari winning this time.* Below right: Sotto voce! *Ferrari people, aware of Gilles's falling oil pressure, implore him to slow down.*

'Know what I remember most about Gilles?' Alan went on. 'I was behind him in the early laps at Monaco in '81, when he was in that awful Ferrari turbo. He was holding me up a bit, and we both knew it. Now, most guys in that situation will just sit there, and be bloody-minded about it, but Gilles was smarter than that. That old tank of his was heavy as hell, and he knew if he stayed ahead of me he soon wasn't going to have any brakes. So he let me by into Mirabeau. By that I mean he left a gap which was about an inch wider than my car! He didn't make it easy, but it was there if I wanted it, and I *knew* that gap wouldn't close once I was into it. Which wasn't true of, say, Piquet. I had trouble later in the race, and Villeneuve repassed me and won. And the greatest compliment I can pay him is to say that, while I wasn't exactly delirious with joy, if it had to happen, I was glad he was the one to benefit from it.'

Jones considers the Montreal race with Villeneuve as perhaps the best victory of his career, and Frank Williams agrees. 'I was very proud of Alan that day. We had the best car at the time, without a doubt, and the only driver on the track we feared was that little French Canadian...'

Watkins Glen was wet, in varying degrees. When the rain was at its worst, Villeneuve's Michelin-shod Ferrari held comfortable sway, but as it eased Jones, Williams and Goodyear came into their own. The battle ended at two-thirds distance, when Alan lost a wheel, improperly secured after a tyre stop; otherwise the Australian would surely have won, for in the late laps Gilles was cruising, keeping a frantic eye on plummeting oil pressure. Even so, he beat Arnoux's Renault by close to a minute.

It is not the race, however, which sticks in the minds of most who went to the Glen in '79. Anyone there for the opening day of qualifying saw conditions perhaps worse than any in living memory. Frankly, it was folly to allow the cars out in such torrential weather, and many drivers stayed in the pits, comparatively snug in their anoraks. But Villeneuve adored driving in the wet.

I watched with Jacques Laffite as a burly Ferrari mechanic carried the tiny helmeted figure across the river in the pits, and deposited him in the cockpit of the T4. '*Gilles*!' Jacques exclaimed. 'He's going out!' And he rubbed his hands in anticipation, calling out to everyone around that they should come and watch.

That afternoon Villeneuve was *eleven seconds* faster than team-mate Scheckter, who was himself well clear of anyone else. Laffite was actually moved by the spectacle: 'Look at him,' he murmured, as the Ferrari skittered by one more time at some unimaginable speed. 'He's different from the rest of us – on a separate level.'

Overleaf: *Image of '79. Scheckter's Ferrari won the World Championship, but it was Villeneuve's which set the pace and wrote the headlines.*

BMW
OFFICIAL CAMERA
Canon
BOSCH
Spark Plugs
TOYOTA
OFFICIAL CAMERA
Canon
12
HEUER

1
+95
SPORTS TIMING
HEUER
TOYOTA

21

12
MICHELIN
Agip

Above right: *Buenos Aires 1980. The start of a desultory year with Ferrari's outdated and outpaced T5. For all that, Gilles got the car up to second before crashing when the front suspension collapsed.*

In Belgium (right) *Villeneuve, whose T5 was out-qualified by such as Daly's Tyrrell, drove flat out all afternoon to finish only sixth.*

Overleaf: *After their successes in 1979, Gilles and Jody suffered the relative ignominy of midfield the following year. The name of the game was downforce, and that they didn't have.*

Marlboro
Marlboro
Agip

Marlboro
Labatt
SMEG
LONGINES
Agip
2
MICHELIN

At Imola, in practice for the Italian Grand Prix, Villeneuve ran Ferrari's new 126 turbo (right), *qualifying it faster than the T5* (below right, *following Arnoux's Renault) which he used in the race.*

Separate level or not, Gilles had a miserable time of it the following year. Essentially, what you needed in 1980 was a first-rate sliding-skirt system – *downforce*. Ferrari's T5, merely an update of the T4, was a better car than its predecessor, but no kind of match for Williams or Brabham or Ligier. And on the fast circuits Renault proved beyond doubt that a turbo was the thing to have.

In many ways, though, Villeneuve's racing personality was never seen to greater effect than in that hapless season of 1980. It is not easy to accept a slide from front-runner to midfield in succeeding years, but Gilles never compromised his quite extraordinary competitiveness. The T5, virtually devoid of downforce, had a fierce hunger for Michelins, yet Villeneuve's tactic remained the same: charge; change tyres; charge all over again – all in the hope of a point or two.

It would have broken the spirit of most men, and Scheckter never sought to disguise his own lack of motivation. By mid-season he had announced he would retire at the end of the year. 'If I hadn't been going to stop anyway,' he says, 'that car would have made the decision for me. It was diabolical! In Canada I didn't qualify, and even Gilles only just made it.'

Shortly before, at Imola, Jody had suffered a huge accident in practice, which brought home to him even more the staring face of mortality. And the race gave Villeneuve cause for similar thoughts. On the flat-out approach to Tosa, his right-rear tyre exploded, pitching the Ferrari off the road and into the bank, from where it rebounded back into the pack.

By some trick of the light everyone missed him, but for Gilles the moment was sober and terrifying. So violent had been the initial impact that for a minute or so he could see nothing. 'I can't describe the fear I felt – that I'd been blinded. The car bounced back into the road, and I could hear all other cars around me, but not see them. I was sitting there, just waiting to be T-boned...'

Happily, the mists began to clear as he was helped from the car, and a check at the track hospital revealed no serious injury. 'I had a terrible headache, and wasn't allowed to fly the helicopter for 24 hours, which was a nuisance, but afterwards I thought a lot about that shunt.

'I'd hit barriers hard before,' Gilles said, 'and once I'd broken my leg in a Formula Atlantic race. After that I was never frightened of it – I thought, you know, you maybe get some fractures, go to the hospital, and they mend you. I'd only ever thought of accidents in terms of broken bones. But being blind maybe...Jesus, that was something I'd never considered.'

Overleaf: *Ferrari's predicament was clearly seen at Brands Hatch, where Villeneuve qualified only 19th, Scheckter 23rd. For all that, Gilles drove as hard as ever – until his engine mercifully let go.*

MICHELIN MICHEL
Agip
2
arexons SKF
MICHELIN MICHELIN
parmalat
6
Marlboro
23
Marlboro
RENAULT elf
elf
FERODO
16
TISSOT
europcar
MICHELIN

LONGINES

MICHELIN
MICHELIN
SMEG
Villeneuve
FIAT
2
MAGNETI MARELLI
Agip
personal
pininfarina
arexons
SKF
speedline

FIAT
BROOKLYN CHEWING GUM
BROOKLYN
Agip
Marlboro
LONGINES
LONGINES
Agip
2

'What the hell are we doing this for?' For Scheckter and Villeneuve, first and second in the '79 World Championship, 1980 was a year to endure. Jody retired at the end of it.

Earlier that weekend he had been in very fine spirits, for Ferrari's first turbocharged car, the 126CK, had made its public debut in qualifying. Its appearance was agricultural, its handling wayward, but of horsepower there was clearly no lack. Villeneuve set his best time with the car, but it was decided he should run the old T5 in the race. He had good thoughts about 1981, although he regretted Scheckter's departure from the scene.

'I don't really know Didier Pironi,' he said, when his new team-mate's appointment was announced. 'I guess I'd been hoping we would have Prost – he's a good fellow with a brilliant talent. But people tell me Pironi is easy to get along with.'

Such proved to be the case, although life must have been a little daunting for Didier in his early days at Maranello. There is no doubt the Frenchman, after several awesome performances for Ligier in 1980, moved camp in the belief he was now the fastest driver in the world. The swift realisation that this was not so must have been difficult for one of his detached *hauteur* to accept.

Pironi was a quiet man, one who always insisted the world had him wrong: he was not arrogant, he argued, but merely shy. And Villeneuve liked him well enough, expressing a trust in him which Joann never shared. From the outset she was wary of Didier Pironi, and this ultimately Gilles would come to remember.

Through 1981, though, there was no hint of a problem between the two Ferrari drivers. Pironi quickly appreciated the degree of adoration everyone felt for Villeneuve, and never showed any outward sign of resentment. 'Gilles has been great to me,' he said when I interviewed him at Hockenheim that year. 'He made me feel welcome here, and we exchange all information. This is his team, really, but we're treated absolutely as equals. On the personal side, we have a lot of things in common. Our characters are very similar.'

Hmm.

Whatever may have been lacking in Pironi the man, however, there was little awry with the racing driver. 'He wasn't a match for Gilles,' Alain Prost remembers, 'but he wasn't often crushed by him, either. People tend to forget, I think, how great a driver Pironi was.'

True enough. At Imola, early in the season, Villeneuve took the pole, and led until a couple of ill-timed tyre stops dropped him down the field; but when that happened his team-mate was well able to lead the rest before slowing with tyre problems in the closing laps. This was a formidable pair.

Gilles's pole position was only the second of his Formula 1 career, which says every-

Marlboro
boro
MICHELIN
Labatt

Zolder 1981. The Ferrari 126CK had an appalling chassis, but excellent horsepower. Left: *Villeneuve leads de Angelis's Lotus on the way to fourth place.*

Not exactly svelte, Ferrari's first turbo car. In the rains of Rio (above) *Gilles ran in the top six before retiring with a broken wastegate.*

Marlboro
WORLD CHAMPIONSHIP TEAM
Ferrari

Villeneuve's Formula 1 debut came at the British Grand Prix in 1977. It was the only time he would appear in a car other than a Ferrari; in the McLaren M23 he was remarkably swift, aggressive and assured.

Marlboro
Agip
HEUER
21

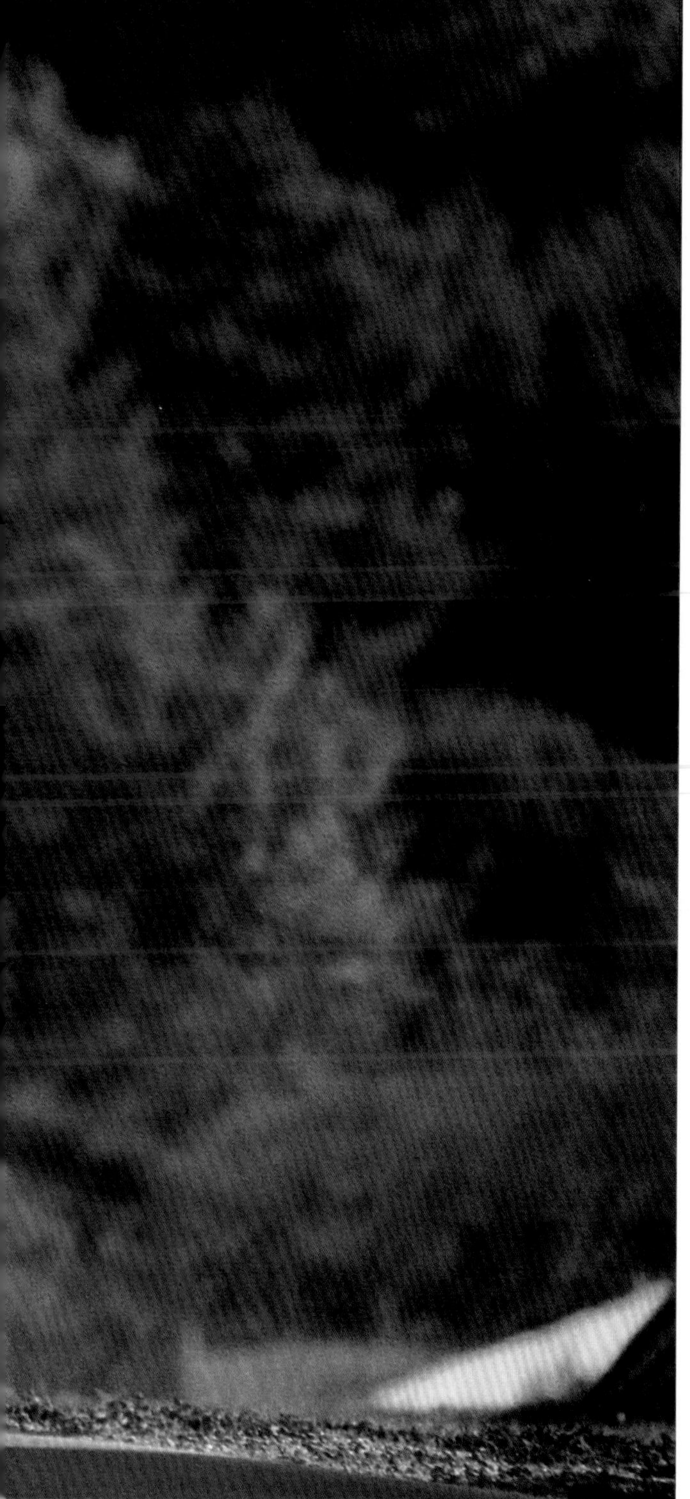

The early races with Ferrari were daunting. Gilles found the T2 wayward and unforgiving, retiring at Mosport (main picture), *and crashing catastrophically at Fuji* (above). *In Italy there were suggestions that Enzo Ferrari would have second thoughts about his new man, but the* Ingegnere *was wiser than that.*

Villeneuve often said he wished he could relive his first Grand Prix victory, at Montreal in late 1978. The outpouring of public emotion rather overwhelmed him, and the aftermath of the win (above) *remained blurred in his mind.*

Marlboro
Labatt
FIAT
Gilles Villeneuve

Shell
MICHELIN
12
Agip
Gilles Villeneuve
12
HEUER

MICHELIN
MICHELIN
LAMBRUSCO WINES MODENA
1978

The Ferrari T4 made its debut at Kyalami in 1979, and Villeneuve (left) *drove a perfect race in wet–dry conditions, winning his second Grand Prix.* Below left: *Gilles beat Jody Scheckter on his home turf, but there was no animosity from the South African. The two men were firm friends.*

The combative spirit of Gilles Villeneuve was never seen to better advantage than at Dijon in 1979, when he alone took on the Renaults, leading them for much of the way and splitting them at the finish.

Below: *In mixed conditions Villeneuve was brilliant at Watkins Glen in '79, fighting with Alan Jones until the Australian's retirement, then babying the Ferrari to the finish with almost zero oil pressure.*

Above right: *At Zandvoort that year Gilles passed Jones's Williams on the* outside *of Tarzan! The controversial drive back to the pits on three wheels* (right) *was conducted at an unlikely speed.*

Marlboro
Marlboro
MICHELIN
Agip
27
MICHELIN
Agip
12
12
12
arexons
MICHELIN

In the 1980 Monaco Grand Prix Villeneuve's T5 ate tyres, as usual, dropping him down the field. In the rain, towards the end of the race, he routinely lapped five seconds faster than anyone else.

Above: *All in all, 1980 was a season to forget…*

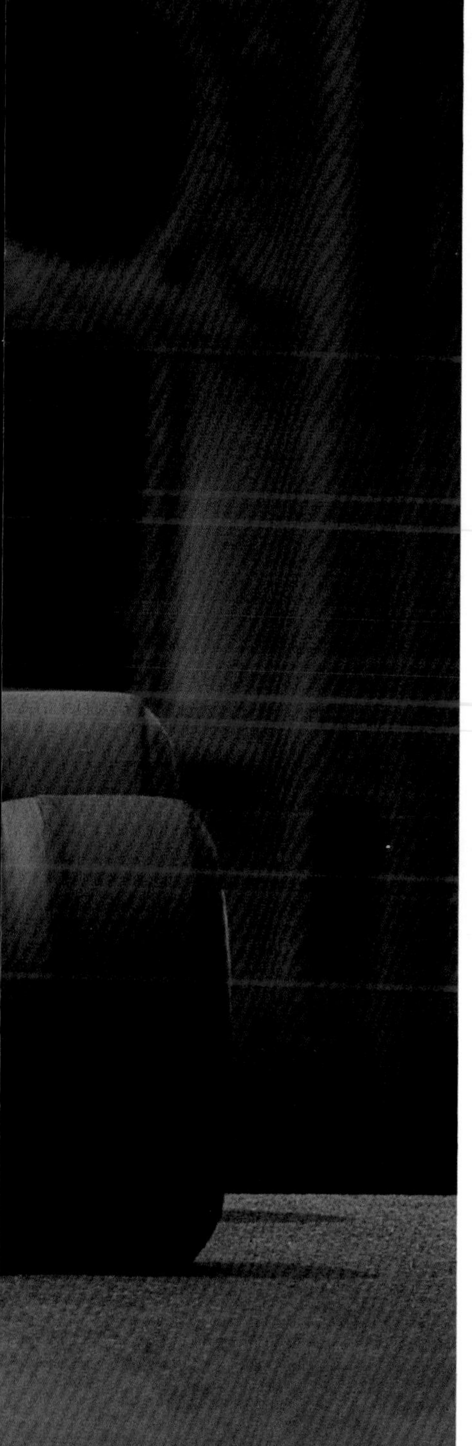

Overleaf: *If Jones had been without problems, Villeneuve would not have won at Monaco in 1981. But a misfire slowed the Williams driver, and Gilles passed him four laps from the end. 'If anyone had to benefit,' Alan said, 'I'm glad it was him…'*

MICHELIN

livetti
MART
FIAT
Agip

The train at Járama in 1981. At the finish Villeneuve, Laffite, Reutemann, Watson and de Angelis were covered by little more than a second. 'That Ferrari had no grip at all,' said a watching Gordon Murray. 'Villeneuve's was the greatest drive I have ever seen…'

SAVA
PEGAS
27

Top: *A great racing driver, and a good man*. Above:
At Zolder, shortly before the last accident.

thing about the cars he was given to drive, for by common consent he was the fastest driver in the business.

It might be argued, though, that he effectively took a third at Monte Carlo, since the cumbersome 126CK was out-qualified only by Piquet's Brabham BT49, a car infinitely more suited to street fighting – and one, moreover, believed to be some considerable way beneath the minimum weight limit.

Villeneuve was magnificent at Monaco that weekend, hustling the cranky Ferrari ever closer to the barriers, and completely psyching Pironi, who hit them three times in his efforts to keep in touch. For the race they lined up second and 17th.

It was Piquet, Villeneuve, Jones after 15 laps, but soon after came the moment to which Alan referred earlier: Gilles let him through. 'There was no sense in trying to keep him back – I would have cooked my brakes. And he was obviously quicker, anyway.'

It was not a wholly altruistic decision, however. 'In race conditions, there was no way I could run with Piquet or Jones, so I figured it might be a good idea to let them get on with it. They hate each other, those two, and at the time things were particularly bad between them...'

So indeed they were. At Zolder, two weeks earlier, Nelson had accused Alan of pushing him off the road – although he was smart enough not to do it to his face. But all manner of dark threats had been made by the Brazilian, and his antipodean rival was keen to get on terms, if possible to humiliate him. The Williams closed right up on the Brabham, and in those circumstances Piquet's composure disintegrated. Not long afterwards he was in the fence, leaving Mr Jones in both the lead and hysterics.

The pattern seemed set now, but with only a dozen or so laps to go the Williams swiftly pitted for attention to a worsening intermittent misfire. Alan rejoined without losing the lead, but the problem remained, and he could do nothing to resist attack from Gilles, the old adversary. Past the pits the Ferrari went ahead, Jones leaving the narrowest of gaps, just as Villeneuve had done earlier.

The win was inherited, yes, but went to a car which had no business on the same lap as a Williams or a Brabham. Pironi's, indeed, was not.

In the camper, two hours later, Gilles looked as if he had been in a war. This was the year of the infamous hydraulic suspension systems, conceived quite cynically to circumvent a new FISA rule calling for a six-centimetre gap between bodywork and ground. At rest, the cars complied; once out on the track, they visibly – and illegally – sank. The whole saga was farcical.

And dangerous, too. To keep their precious skirts (now fixed) from swift disintegra-

tion, engineers went to ever stiffer springs, to the point that the cars now had no discernible suspension movement. Horrible to drive, even painful to experience.

'Right now I'm sore everywhere,' Villeneuve said. 'Monaco is tiring, anyway, but this ridiculous go-kart ride we all have now makes it worse than ever. *Bang, bang, bang*! All the way through my helmet was smashing into the roll-over bar.

'What worries me more', he went on, 'is what's happening to the cars. The suspension is taking a hell of a beating, and think of what's going through the tyre sidewalls...'

It was a supreme irony, in fact, that through the last year or so of his life Gilles, always known as the bravest of the brave, expressed his fears of racing's unnecessary dangers more than any other driver. Like nearly all his colleagues, he detested the ground-effect cars, and it was hardly surprising: apart from their complete lack of feel, the crude technique they required militated against the great driver. Talent was impotent in the face of downforce.

Joann joins Gilles on the rostrum at Monte Carlo (left) *after his first victory in two years, one which nobody had anticipated.*

The 126CK, with its unmannerly chassis and on-or-off power delivery, was scarcely ideal for the streets of Monaco (above)*, but Villeneuve was faultless on race day.*

Monaco 1981. Villeneuve blasts out of the tunnel, in apparently vain pursuit of Jones's Williams. When the Australian's car faltered, late in the race, Gilles was on hand to benefit, his charge rewarded.

Labatt
MICHELIN
Agip
olivetti

MICHELIN
FLY
saudia
CS
LUBRICANTES
Marlboro
Firestone
Leyland
FIAT
TALBOT
27

Járama 1981. It was very hot that day, and afterwards Villeneuve – whose stamina was always high – looked, and felt, completely spent.

At Járama, two weeks later, Villeneuve won again, once more flouting the run of play in Formula 1. He qualified only seventh, but even that flattered the Ferrari at this, a circuit which always favoured grip over horsepower.

After qualifying he was despondent: 'I don't think I was ever this disappointed with the T5. We have a fantastic engine, the best facilities, Fiorano and all the rest of it – and this chassis is *terrible*! You put on new tyres, and it's OK for four laps. After that, forget it. It's just like a fast, red Cadillac, wallowing all over the place.'

He shrugged in resignation, but then back came the grin. 'The amazing thing about the chassis is that it's so forgiving. I can get so sideways I'm almost looking over the roll-over bar – and still it comes back! But I'd sooner have it vicious, with some grip.'

At the start he played his high card to perfection. There was no secret to his technique away from the grid, he insisted: it was simply a matter of keeping the revs at a steady 11,000, then slipping your foot sideways off the clutch when the green light flashed. Wasn't that what everyone did?

Given the Ferrari's acceleration, you needed to be alert in the opening seconds, for others around you were not going forward at the same rate. Before the first turn, Gilles found a path by Giacomelli, Prost, Watson and Laffite. Only the Williamses of Jones and Reutemann were ahead, and at the end of the first lap he powered past Carlos.

Alan, though, was gone. And had he not most untypically gone off the road on lap 14 the 1981 Spanish Grand Prix would not have passed into motor racing legend. For the next 66 laps Villeneuve would face unremitting pressure, first from Reutemann, then from Laffite.

The closing stages were unforgettable. In tandem circulated Gilles, Jacques, Carlos and two late additions to the game, John Watson and Elio de Angelis. Ferrari led Ligier, Williams, McLaren and Lotus.

The Ferrari was hopeless through the Spanish circuit's tight corners, but Gilles used its power on the main straight to stay in front. Above left: *Most of the pressure came from Reutemann, but in the late laps* (left) *pole man Laffite took his place behind Villeneuve, who scored his most unexpected victory.*

Shell Super Oil
Shell Super Oil
Shell Super Oil
Mobil Mobil Mobil
DUNLOP
DUNLOP
TOYOTA
Shell Super Oil
Lucas
FERODO
ESSO
Mobil

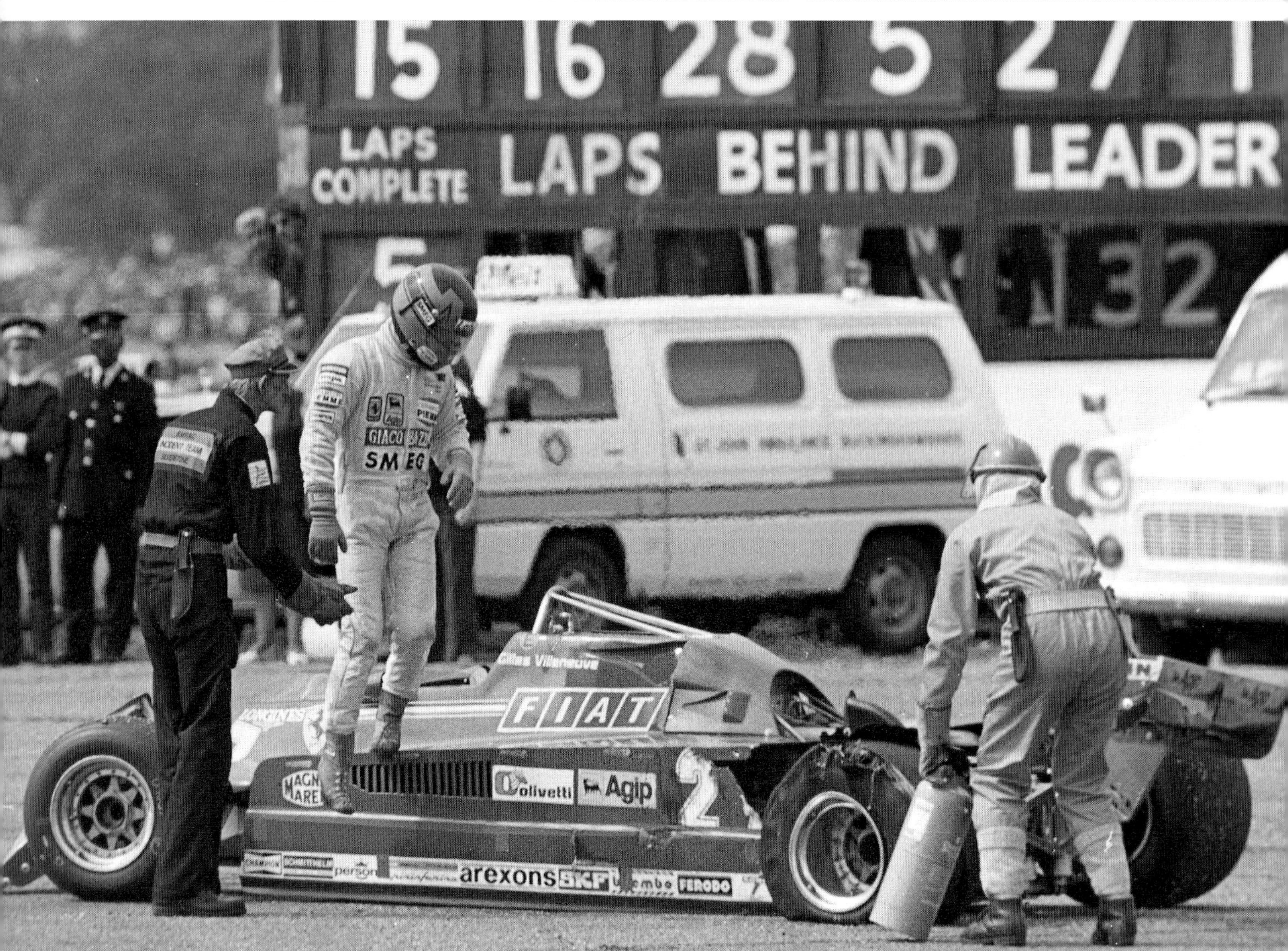
15 16 28 5 27 1
LAPS COMPLETE
LAPS BEHIND LEADER
32
SMEG
Gilles Villeneuve
FIAT
Olivetti
Agip
arexons
SKF
FERODO

In the British Grand Prix Villeneuve's car tagged the Woodcote kerbing, which bounced the Ferrari into a spin (left). *Jones's Williams and de Cesaris's McLaren were also eliminated.* Below left: *Gilles set off again in the hobbled 126CK, but pulled off before the end of the lap.*

Gordon Murray walked the circuit that afternoon. Bored with confinement to the pits, he wanted to watch a race from the trackside, and a good one he chose. 'That', he remarked afterwards, 'is the greatest drive I have ever seen by any driver. You can't believe how evil that Ferrari was! With all that pressure on him, Villeneuve never made a single mistake.'

Every lap it was the same. Gilles would pull away down the pit straight, and through Járama's endless tight turns Jacques or Carlos would claw back again. It was that way right to the flag. A second and a bit covered the first five.

Not even two swallows make a summer, however. Monaco and Járama were it for Villeneuve in 1981. At Dijon he retired early in the race, and at Silverstone triggered a multiple accident at the Woodcote chicane. After clipping a kerb, the Ferrari quite literally bounced into a spin, which unfortunately left Jones's Williams with nowhere to go.

At Hockenheim, a circuit he loathed, Villeneuve found the Ferrari way off the pace, and the same was true at the Österreichring, where brake problems put him into the fence at the Boschkurve. 'They put new, harder, pads in for the race,' he grimaced, 'and I guess they would have lasted half a season. What they didn't do was slow the car down very much...'

By Monza Gilles was plainly despondent. Fifth fastest on the opening day, he blew up on his first qualifying run on Saturday. 'I got back to the pits to find there was nothing for me to drive – and we brought four bloody cars here! Yesterday Pironi crashed his race car, and used his spare. Today he says the spare has a vibration – and they give him *my* spare! So there he is, improving his time in my car, and I'm sitting in the pits.'

Add to that the discovery that 'fans' had plundered his helicopter, stealing all the radio equipment and his briefcase, and Villeneuve's temporary disaffection with things Italian was readily understandable. Nor was it diminished when turbo failure put him out of the Italian Grand Prix after only six laps.

At Montreal there was a surreptitious approach from Ron Dennis: would Villeneuve go to McLaren for 1982, as team-mate to the returning Niki Lauda? Question was, how to discuss the fiscal arrangements at the track, without revealing anything to Ferrari's Marco Piccinini, hawk-eyed and hovering as ever? They hit on the idea of using pit boards.

So it was that, between sessions, Dennis casually put 2.5 (million dollars) on the McLaren board. Whereupon Gilles sauntered over, removed the 2 and substituted a 3...

Piccinini was onto it like a shot. What was Villeneuve playing at? 'Oh,' Gilles said,

Right: *Gilles never showed much interest in flying aeroplanes, but helicopters quickly became a passion.*

'just a private joke with McLaren...' And Marco, amazingly, bought it.

It is fascinating to contemplate the what-might-have-been aspect of Villeneuve in a John Barnard car. He was certainly tempted; indeed he had earlier that season spoken to Frank Williams about a possible move. At heart, though, Gilles was the prisoner of Ferrari – he always *wanted* to believe things would come right with his beloved red cars. 'I'm hopeless,' he laughed on one occasion when we spoke of it. 'I get really pissed off, and all my common sense tells me to go to Frank or McLaren, and then I go and see the Old Man, and I'm lost...'

Still, it seemed there was good cause for optimism about 1982. Harvey Postlethwaite had gone to Maranello, and the combination of Ferrari horsepower in an 'English' chassis looked irresistible. On paper, at least. Through that winter Villeneuve's spirits were particularly high.

Professionally, anyway. Less settled now was his marriage, always previously one of the strongest in motor racing. In their early years together Gilles and Joann lived in something close to poverty, as everything was sacrificed to the dream of Formula 1. They were very young when their two children were born, and life was hard for a long time.

Once established as a Grand Prix driver, Villeneuve became rich beyond reverie, and did not stint himself. In the words of Patrick Tambay, perhaps his closest friend: 'Everything in Gilles's life moved at 200 mph, whether it was driving, playing Monopoly, flying helicopters or spending!'

Fortunately, there was always enough money around for this not to be a serious problem but, by his own admission, Gilles and his sometimes fidgety spirit were not always easy to live with, and a sympathy for anything on the same planet as feminism had not been part of his upbringing in rural Quebec.

As well as that, his years in Europe unquestionably changed him. His outward confidence grew, for one thing, although this never manifested itself in arrogance. He was living in a world for which his first 25 years had been no preparation. 'Look at this,' he exclaimed delightedly one day. 'A hick from Berthierville with James Bond!' And indeed there was a photograph of Sean Connery and himself at the Gala Dinner after the Monaco Grand Prix of 1981. He seemed almost to have missed the point that the whole evening had been in his honour, that *he* had won the race, *he* was the star...

Over time his language became ever more salty, and in French, English or Italian he was never afraid to say what he thought, never wary of upsetting a Balestre or Ecclestone. His sense of humour, never far from the surface, was always splendidly irreverent:

Unfamiliar in formal dress (near right), *Villeneuve celebrates his Monaco win with the Stewarts and the Connerys.* Far right: *Gilles and Joann* en route *to the Monaco pits.*

PIEMME

MICHELIN MICHELIN
MICHELIN
FIAT
Gilles Villeneuve
27
LONGINES
27
Agip
olivetti
speedline
SKF
arexons

4

In the early stages at Las Vegas, Villeneuve leads Giacomelli, Laffite and Watson. The Ferrari was later disqualified for a startline infringement.

Montreal 1981. Above left: *In appalling conditions Villeneuve finished third, behind Laffite and Watson. Gilles laps Alboreto's Tyrrell* (left), *the Ferrari's nose now breaking up after contact with de Angelis's Lotus.*

GOOD
27

The Postlethwaite-designed 126C2 looked like the answer for 1982, but in South Africa (left) *turbo failure put Gilles out early, and at Rio* (below left) *he crashed while trying to hold off Piquet's Brabham for the lead.*

he could have you falling about with impressions of people in racing for whom he did not care.

Perhaps Didier Pironi, who had never known anything but wealth and privilege, changed him in ways, too. The Frenchman, at the helm of the short-lived Professional Racing Drivers' Association, was very active in the politics of Formula 1, for one thing; very much a ladies' man, for another. There was much on Villeneuve's mind as 1982 approached.

The racing year began in South Africa, and controversially, too, with a drivers' strike, occasioned by a new FISA form relating to the Superlicence. A couple of clauses therein the drivers found unacceptable. Therefore they skipped the first day of qualifying altogether, instead going off to a hotel in Johannesburg, where they literally barricaded themselves into the ballroom for the night. As dealings with the governing body went on, the drivers staged an impromptu cabaret to pass the time. A variety of 'turns' included a lecture on terrorism from Bruno Giacomelli, and piano playing by Villeneuve (Scott Joplin rags) and the concert-trained Elio de Angelis (Mozart and Beethoven). An evening most of those present recall with affection and pleasure.

Next day they were back at the track, however, where Gilles qualified third behind Arnoux's Renault and Piquet's Brabham-BMW. He was, however, well over a second faster than Pironi. In the race both men retired.

In Brazil the drivers' dissatisfaction with the current cars was at its height. FISA, finally appreciating the absurdity of hydraulic suspension systems, had approved the return of skirts, albeit in fixed form. The rock-hard springs of the year before necessarily remained, therefore, and cornering speeds were becoming ludicrous. Over the bumps of Rio the 1982 Grand Prix cars were nightmarish for their occupants. In practice I spoke at length on the subject with Villeneuve. As ever, he was in no mood to be mealy-mouthed.

We got into it when he asked for a quiet word about Pironi. He was off the pace that weekend, Gilles said, because a recent testing shunt at Ricard had severely shaken him, and his confidence was all to hell. It had been a *big* accident. 'When you write your report,' Gilles asked, 'please go easy on him. He'll be OK by the next race.'

They were words I was to remember a few weeks later. In the normal course of events, a racing driver rarely passes up a chance to score off his team-mate. It was the act of a compassionate and guileless man, and I came to wonder if Didier Pironi ever appreciated the extent of the friendship he was to toss away.

'I think I probably enjoy driving – for its own sake – more than a lot of drivers,'

Villeneuve said. 'But I *hate* these cars. Two or three years ago, I used to enjoy myself at every corner, maybe 15 times a lap. Now I enjoy myself once every 15 laps! No one outside of Formula 1 can know how bad these things are to drive. I'll try and explain how they feel.

'There is a moment, going over a bump and turning into a corner at the same time, when you lose vision. Everything goes blurred. The G-forces are unbelievable now that we have skirts back again. *Incredible*! And it's not like the G-forces in an aeroplane, because in a car they're lateral G-forces, pulling you sideways.

'The steering is ridiculously heavy – like being in a big truck, with the power steering not working. Sometimes you feel you don't have the strength to pull it round a corner.

'And, of course, we have no suspension. Sometimes you go over a bump, and you feel as though someone is kicking you in the back. Your legs are flung around in the cockpit, banging against the steering rack, and your head constantly hits the back of the cockpit or the roll-over bar. After a while your sides ache, your head aches, and you become consciously aware of not enjoying driving a racing car...'

Were we reaching a point where a racing driver's most important qualities were his physical strength and stamina?

'Absolutely.' Gilles was emphatic. 'The days of driving with your fingertips are gone. Now you have to grip the wheel, simply to hold on, to get the car to turn into the corner. A lot of the art has gone out of it – nearly all, in fact.

'The problem is that nothing is being done. Tomorrow, after the race, I know that people will be complaining like hell about fatigue. But then we go to places like Long Beach, Monaco and Imola, where the G-forces will be less, and the matter will be forgotten. Zolder, I guess, will be quite a good killer, and Brands Hatch will be *something else*! And who can imagine how it will be in Austria?'

And were all the drivers in agreement with him on this?

'Yes, for sure, but some of them don't like to say too much about it, either because they are afraid of upsetting their boss, or because they want to play the tough guy. Well, I'll tell you, I think I can play the tough guy as well as anyone, but I'm not afraid to say what I think about these cars.

'The cornering speeds are crazy. More important, though, are the corner *approach* speeds. These days you don't really brake. You lift off the throttle, point the car into the corner, touch the brakes as you go towards the apex. If anything goes wrong – like a jammed throttle – it's too bad. You simply don't have time to do anything about it. Already you're off the road.

'Look at Pironi's testing accident at Ricard. His throttle jammed at 180 mph. The car went through all the catch-fencing, into the guard rail, over it, across the grass, into the spectator fence. He was testing, and there was no one there, but if that had been in the race, he would have killed some spectators, for sure. And, whatever else, we *cannot* risk that.'

Very well, I said: you're the President of FISA. Define your ideal Formula 1 car.

'For me, it's very simple,' he replied. 'I love motor racing. To me it's a sport, not a technical exercise. My ideal Formula 1 car would be something like a McLaren M23, with a big normally aspirated engine, 800 horsepower, 21-inch rear tyres. A lot of people say we should have narrower tyres, but I don't agree, because you need big tyres to slow you down if you spin. And you need a lot of horsepower to unstick big tyres, to make the cars slide.

'That would be a bloody fantastic spectacle, I can tell you. We would take corners one gear lower than we do now, and get the cars sideways. You know, people still rave about Ronnie Peterson in a Lotus 72, and I understand that. I agree with them. That's the kind of entertainment I want to give the crowds. Smoke the tyres! Yeah!'

The fans, the fans.... Very few people in racing seem ever to consider them, I suggested.

'Well, I do, because I used to be one of them! I believe the crowd is really losing out at the moment, and that's bad. OK, we may not get any pleasure from driving these cars, but forget about that. We're paid to do it, and people will say, "Even if it hurts, drive it." I understand that, and if it gave good entertainment to the crowds I'd accept it. But these cars are so boring to watch.

'Spectators like to see cars sliding, but you can't slide them now. First of all, you don't have the balls to do it, because the cars are so twitchy and nervous. Second, the steering is too heavy to give you the delicate control you need to slide. Third, it's not efficient, loses you time.

'So this is crazy, right? The drivers don't like these cars, and neither do the spectators, so who does like them? Well, the aerodynamicists, I guess. But the people don't come to see how good aerodynamicists are – they come to see a battle, a *spectacle*. They come to be stirred, excited. And at the moment they're being cheated.

'If we went round a corner 20 mph slower, the public would barely notice it – particularly if we were cornering in nice power slides. They would like that.'

The conversation then took a turn which would assume an extreme poignancy a few weeks later. You are considered as brave as there is, I said, and safety has never been a subject of primary concern to you. Do the dangers of motor racing worry you more than they did?

'No, not as such. But I object to the fact that so many of the dangers we face are unnecessary, and could be easily removed. I believe the cars are far more dangerous now than they have ever been, although I know they're stronger.

'Forget the cars for a moment,' Villeneuve went on. 'Look at qualifying. It's become a farce. We have two sets of qualifying tyres for each driver in each timed session. Now here, at Rio, qualifiers give you one really quick lap; after that they start to go off. So really you have two opportunities to set your quick time. First of all, you spend very little time on the track, which is again bad for the public, who have nothing to watch. The end of qualifying, with everyone balls out for a last *banzai* lap, used to be really exciting, but not any more.

'Second, qualifying is now unnecessarily dangerous, and I mean "unnecessarily". If I have only two chances to get a good position on the grid, I must wait until the track is clear. I go for my *banzai* lap, and I *need* a clear track. If it isn't clear, if there's someone in my way, I must just hope he's looking in his mirrors. I *cannot* lift, because this is my last chance of a quick lap...'

These were, of course, precisely the circumstances in which Gilles would lose his life. At the time of the Brazilian Grand Prix his disenchantment was such that he was actively considering abandoning Formula 1 until the cars were cars again.

'I guess I'm not thinking of quitting – not *seriously* at the moment, anyway. But I love racing so much it makes me sad to see the sport being spoiled.'

His expression lightened as more pleasing thoughts came into his head. 'At the moment I get a headache every time I drive the car. Now, if you make love to a woman, and at the same time someone sticks a knife in your back, eventually you won't like making love so much, right? In the same way, if you like driving, but feel that your head's being punched every time you come into a corner, eventually you won't like that so much. But...take away the knife, and I still like making love!'

The following day he led from the start, holding off the more wieldy Brabhams and Williamses for a long time, before eventually spinning off on worn tyres. It was the old Villeneuve creed, never once compromised: better to go off in the lead than coast along for two or three safe points.

At Long Beach he was third to Lauda and Rosberg, but was later disqualified for an illegal rear wing. And then came Imola.

Much has been written about that weekend. The FOCA teams, Tyrrell apart, stayed

Long Beach 1982. Top: *Villeneuve spins while trying to outbrake Rosberg's Williams in their scrap for second place. Gilles finally finished third on the road, but that 'trick' rear wing* (above) *got him disqualified…*

Imola was where everything changed. Villeneuve, here leading Pironi, thought he was cruising home to victory. But his team-mate had other ideas and stole the win on the last lap, leaving Gilles no opportunity to respond.

GIACOBAZZI
LAMBRUSCO
GOOD YEAR
RENAULT
Agip
arexons
27

away in protest. Essentially, they had been cheating, and were ordered to stop forthwith, although this of course was not how they saw it. Their absence left what was effectively a four-car race, between the Ferraris and the Renaults.

Villeneuve was relaxed during practice, gabbling eagerly about his new Agusta helicopter, which was parked on a football field nearby. And he was pleased, too, with the Ferrari. While not quite a match for the Renaults, it would enable him to make a race of it on Sunday. In qualifying he was 1.4 seconds faster than Pironi. The two men, and their wives, had dinner together on Saturday evening.

The following day Gilles took the fight to the Renaults, his team-mate content to sit behind. And when the French cars duly blew up, the massive crowd rapturously prepared for Villeneuve's first Italian victory. He had earned it, and it was also in keeping with traditional Ferrari team orders: the man ahead when the red cars become first and second is the man ahead at the flag.

They had but 16 laps to run, and now the only worry was going the distance: on fuel the Ferraris were marginal at this, the thirstiest circuit in Formula 1.

Accordingly, Gilles backed off, and he was not too concerned when Pironi went in front for a while. It was, after all, merely a show for the crowds. Wasn't it?

What was a little disquieting, though, was that Pironi tended to pick up the pace whenever he was ahead, as if oblivious of the fuel problem. So Villeneuve went to the front again, and slowed them once more.

Seven laps left – and it was Pironi ahead again, where he stayed for quite a while. This *was* a game, wasn't it? From the Ferrari pits there were anxious signals every time around, reminding the drivers it would be a bad thing for the two cars to run dry on the last lap in Italy.

Into the last lap, though, Villeneuve led once more, and everyone relaxed. It *had* been showmanship, nothing more. Down the straight to Tosa the red cars were cruising. But as they approached the corner Pironi sprinted by, catching his team-mate completely unawares. The Frenchman, indeed, carved right across Villeneuve's bows, and the two cars very nearly touched.

It was the last overtaking spot on the circuit, and suddenly Gilles realised he had been duped. No chance to get on terms remained, and when they crossed the line it was 28 from 27.

After a furious slowing-down lap, Villeneuve brought his car into the paddock, slewing it to a stop after a final burst of throttle. As he stepped out, removed his helmet and balaclava, his face was quietly livid. A single word – English, and of four letters – summed

The Ferrari crew celebrate their 1–2 at Imola, unaware of what has happened out on the track. They would know soon enough.

Gilles came up to the Imola rostrum only briefly, and his expression (above) tells its own story. Top: Pironi, claiming he had been in a fair fight, tells the press all about it.

up his feelings for his team-mate. He did not accompany Pironi and third man Alboreto on the lap of honour.

On the rostrum his expression said it all. This was farce, nothing less, and after a token appearance he left for the park where his helicopter awaited. One of those joining him on the flight was Jackie Stewart.

'I had never seen Gilles angry like that,' Stewart recalls. 'You know, with him the World Championship was incidental. He told me that evening his one goal was to beat my record, win more races than I had. And this one had been stolen from him. He was *stunned*. There had always been this innocence about Gilles – he didn't have a trace of maliciousness in him. And he couldn't quite believe what had happened to him that day. It was awful that the last days of his life were so tormented and disillusioned.'

Villeneuve left the track before I had a chance to speak to him, so I waited a couple of days, then called the apartment in Monte Carlo. We talked for an hour and more, and afterwards I felt disturbed and apprehensive.

Before leaving the circuit, I had collected all the time sheets, as usual. When Villeneuve led, the Ferraris were lapping in 1m 37s–1m 38s, but when Pironi was in front the times came down to 1m 35s. This tallied precisely with Gilles's version; the truth always tallies. Not until the last half of the last lap had he realised he was in a race.

'I think I've proved, you know, in the 60-odd Grands Prix I've done so far, that in equal cars – or even sometimes in a lesser car – when I want someone to stay behind...I think he stays behind. No *way* would he have passed me, and nor would anyone else. Not on the last lap...

'Finishing second is one thing – I would have been mad at myself for not being quick enough if he'd beaten me. But finishing second because the bastard steals it...Jesus, that's why I'm mad. Everyone seemed to think we had the fight of our lives, which is a *joke*! The first two or three times he came inside and passed, I thought, well, he wants to play a little bit, and I never defended myself. But him, he was just racing, and I was too stupid to realise it. I thought he was an honest guy. Joann was right about him all along.'

Had he made his feelings clear to Pironi?

'No,' Gilles answered. 'I haven't spoken to him since, and I'm not going to speak to him again – ever. I have declared war on him. I've told Piccinini I'll work inside the team, just like before, but no more co-operation with him. If the engineers want to pass on to him what I say about the car, that's up to them. But I'll do my own thing in future. When we get to Belgium next week I'll race with him as if he had a Williams

Zolder. In the paddock Gilles talks to Niki Lauda, who had become a close friend. The great Austrian was deeply affected by the accident later in the day, and paid generous tribute to Villeneuve, as man and driver.

or Brabham...'

The furies were still inside him on the Friday at Zolder. After practice I went into the pit to speak to him. 'Let's get out of here,' he said when Pironi drove in.

I had written a lengthy column for *Autosport*, based on our telephone conversation of the week before, and gave him a copy. It was entitled 'Bad Blood in Maranello', and after the following morning's session Gilles thanked me for it. He was calmer now, chatty and himself again. Mauro Forghieri came over, slapped him on the back. And I left them to it, went off to argue with Teddy Mayer.

'Gilles was a perfect racing driver, I think,' Niki Lauda said the next morning. 'He had the best talent of all of us. In any car he was quick. He didn't drive for points, but to win races. I liked him even more than I admired him. He was the best – and the fastest – racing driver in the world.'

Right: *Atlantic days in Canada: Gilles, with rivals Bill Brack and Howdy Holmes.*

GILLES VILLENEUVE · CAREER RECORD
BY JOHN TAYLOR

1974

	Race	Circuit	Date	Entrant	Car	Comment
3	Player's Formula Atlantic Challenge	Westwood	26/05/74	Ecurie Canada	March 74B-Ford BDA	
22	Player's Formula Atlantic Challenge	Edmonton	02/06/74	Ecurie Canada	March 74B-Ford BDA	
ret	Player's Formula Atlantic Challenge	Gimli	16/06/74	Ecurie Canada	March 74B-Ford BDA	*engine*
ret	Player's Formula Atlantic Challenge	Mosport Park	01/07/74	Ecurie Canada	March 74B-Ford BDA	*accident/fractured leg*
7	Player's Formula Atlantic Challenge	Halifax	11/08/74	Ecurie Canada	March 74B-Ford BDA	
ret	Molson Grand Prix	Trois Rivières	01/09/74	Ecurie Canada	March 74B-Ford BDA	*accident*

1975

	Race	Circuit	Date	Entrant	Car	Comment
15	Player's Formula Atlantic Challenge	Edmonton	25/05/75	Equipe Villeneuve/Skiroule	March 75B-Ford BDA	
5	Player's Formula Atlantic Challenge	Westwood	01/06/75	Equipe Villeneuve/Skiroule	March 75B-Ford BDA	
1	Player's Formula Atlantic Challenge	Gimli	22/06/75	Equipe Villeneuve/Skiroule	March 75B-Ford BDA	
2	Player's Formula Atlantic Challenge	St Jovite	06/07/75	Equipe Villeneuve/Skiroule	March 75B-Ford BDA	*Fastest lap*
17	Player's Formula Atlantic Challenge	Mosport Park	20/07/75	Equipe Villeneuve/Skiroule	March 75B-Ford BDA	
14	Player's Formula Atlantic Challenge	Halifax	17/08/75	Equipe Villeneuve/Skiroule	March 75B-Ford BDA	
ret	Molson Grand Prix	Trois Rivières	31/08/75	Equipe Villeneuve/Skiroule	March 75B-Ford BDA	*brakes*
4	Formula Atlantic Race	Donnybrooke	07/09/75	Equipe Villeneuve/Skiroule	March 75B-Ford BDA	

1976

	Race	Circuit	Date	Entrant	Car	Comment
ret	Daytona 24 Hours	Daytona	31/01-01/02/76	Mo Carter	Chevrolet Camaro	*engine/c/d Mo Carter*
1	IMSA Formula Atlantic Championship	Road Atlanta	11/04/76	Ecurie Canada	March 76B-Ford BDA	*Pole*
1	IMSA Formula Atlantic Championship	Laguna Seca	02/05/76	Ecurie Canada	March 76B-Ford BDA	
1	IMSA Formula Atlantic Championship	Ontario Speedway	09/05/76	Ecurie Canada	March 76B-Ford BDA	*Pole/Fastest lap*
1	Player's Formula Atlantic Challenge	Edmonton	16/05/76	Ecurie Canada	March 76B-Ford BDA	*Pole/Fastest lap*
ret	Player's Formula Atlantic Challenge	Westwood	30/05/76	Ecurie Canada	March 76B-Ford BDA	*Pole/accident/engine cut out*
ret	Pau Grand Prix (F2)	Pau	07/06/76	Project 4 Racing	March 762-Hart	*overheating*
1	Player's Formula Atlantic Challenge	Gimli	13/06/76	Ecurie Canada	March 76B-Ford BDA	*Pole*
1	Player's Formula Atlantic Challenge	St Jovite	11/07/76	Ecurie Canada	March 76B-Ford BDA	*Pole/Fastest lap*
1	Player's Formula Atlantic Challenge	Halifax	08/08/76	Ecurie Canada	March 76B-Ford BDA	*Fastest lap*
1	Molson Grand Prix	Trois Rivières	05/09/76	Ecurie Canada	March 76B-Ford BDA	*Pole/Fastest lap*
1	IMSA Formula Atlantic Championship	Road Atlanta	19/09/76	Ecurie Canada	March 76B-Ford BDA	*Pole/Fastest lap*

1977

3	Philips Formula Atlantic Race	Roy Hesketh	15/01/77	Valvoline	Chevron B39-Ford BDA	
5	Philips Formula Atlantic Race	Kyalami	29/01/77	Valvoline	Chevron B39-Ford BDA	
8	Philips Formula Atlantic Race	Welkom	05/02/77	Valvoline	Chevron B39-Ford BDA	*long pit stop*
ret	Philips Formula Atlantic Race	Killarney	19/02/77	Valvoline	Chevron B39-Ford BDA	*collision with Ian Scheckter*
2	Labatt's Formula Atlantic Challenge	Mosport Park	22/05/77	Ecurie Canada	March 77B-Ford BDA	*Pole/Fastest lap*
ret	Labatt's Formula Atlantic Challenge	Gimli	26/06/77	Ecurie Canada	March 77B-Ford BDA	*engine*
1	Labatt's Formula Atlantic Challenge	Edmonton	03/07/77	Ecurie Canada	March 77B-Ford BDA	*Pole*
ret	Watkins Glen Can-Am	Watkins Glen	10/07/77	Walter Wolf Racing	Wolf Dallara WD1-Chevrolet	*gear linkage*
11	BRITISH GP	Silverstone	16/07/77	Marlboro Team McLaren	McLaren M23-Cosworth DFV	*pit stop*
3	Elkhart Lake Can-Am	Elkhart Lake	24/07/77	Walter Wolf Racing	Wolf Dallara WD1-Chevrolet	
ret	Labatt's Formula Atlantic Challenge	Halifax	07/08/77	Ecurie Canada	March 77B-Ford BDA	*Pole/accident*
1	Labatt's Formula Atlantic Challenge	St Felicien	14/08/77	Ecurie Canada	March 77B-Ford BDA	*Pole*
3	Molson Diamond 6 Hours	Mosport Park	20/08/77	BMW Canada	BMW 320i	*c/d Eddie Cheever*
ret	Mosport Park Can-Am	Mosport Park	21/08/77	Walter Wolf Racing	Wolf Dallara WD1-Chevrolet	*broken wheel*
ret	Trois Rivières Can-Am	Trois Rivières	04/09/77	Walter Wolf Racing	Wolf Dallara WD1-Chevrolet	*broken gear linkage*
4	Molson Grand Prix	Trois Rivières	04/09/77	Ecurie Canada	March 77B-Ford BDA	*Pole*
1	Labatt's Formula Atlantic Challenge	Quebec	25/09/77	Ecurie Canada	March 77B-Ford BDA	
12/*ret*	CANADIAN GP	Mosport Park	09/10/77	Scuderia Ferrari SpA SEFAC	Ferrari 312T2	*driveshaft*
ret	JAPANESE GP	Mount Fuji	23/10/77	Scuderia Ferrari SpA SEFAC	Ferrari 312T2	*accident/hit Peterson*

1978

8	ARGENTINE GP	Buenos Aires	15/01/78	Scuderia Ferrari SpA SEFAC	Ferrari 312T2	
ret	BRAZILIAN GP	Rio	29/01/78	Scuderia Ferrari SpA SEFAC	Ferrari 312T2	*spun off*
ret	SOUTH AFRICAN GP	Kyalami	04/03/78	Scuderia Ferrari SpA SEFAC	Ferrari 312T3	*oil leak*
ret	US GP WEST	Long Beach	02/04/78	Scuderia Ferrari SpA SEFAC	Ferrari 312T3	*collision with Regazzoni*
ret	MONACO GP	Monte Carlo	07/05/78	Scuderia Ferrari SpA SEFAC	Ferrari 312T3	*tyre failure/accident*
4	BELGIAN GP	Zolder	21/05/78	Scuderia Ferrari SpA SEFAC	Ferrari 312T3	
10	SPANISH GP	Járama	04/06/78	Scuderia Ferrari SpA SEFAC	Ferrari 312T3	*pit stop/tyres*
9	SWEDISH GP	Anderstorp	17/06/78	Scuderia Ferrari SpA SEFAC	Ferrari 312T3	*pit stop/tyres*
12	FRENCH GP	Paul Ricard	02/07/78	Scuderia Ferrari SpA SEFAC	Ferrari 312T3	*pit stops/tyres*
ret	BRITISH GP	Brands Hatch	16/07/78	Scuderia Ferrari SpA SEFAC	Ferrari 312T3	*driveshaft*
8	GERMAN GP	Hockenheim	30/07/78	Scuderia Ferrari SpA SEFAC	Ferrari 312T3	*pit stop/tyres*
3	AUSTRIAN GP	Österreichring	13/08/78	Scuderia Ferrari SpA SEFAC	Ferrari 312T3	
6	DUTCH GP	Zandvoort	27/08/78	Scuderia Ferrari SpA SEFAC	Ferrari 312T3	
7	ITALIAN GP	Monza	10/09/78	Scuderia Ferrari SpA SEFAC	Ferrari 312T3	*2nd on road/1-min. penalty*
ret	US GP EAST	Watkins Glen	01/10/78	Scuderia Ferrari SpA SEFAC	Ferrari 312T3	*engine*
1	CANADIAN GP	Montreal	08/10/78	Scuderia Ferrari SpA SEFAC	Ferrari 312T3	

1979

ret	ARGENTINE GP	Buenos Aires	21/01/79	Scuderia Ferrari SpA SEFAC	Ferrari 312T3	*engine*
5	BRAZILIAN GP	Interlagos	04/02/79	Scuderia Ferrari SpA SEFAC	Ferrari 312T3	
1	SOUTH AFRICAN GP	Kyalami	03/03/79	Scuderia Ferrari SpA SEFAC	Ferrari 312T4	*Fastest lap*
1	US GP WEST	Long Beach	08/04/79	Scuderia Ferrari SpA SEFAC	Ferrari 312T4	*Pole/Fastest lap*
1	Race of Champions	Brands Hatch	15/04/79	Scuderia Ferrari SpA SEFAC	Ferrari 312T3	
7	SPANISH GP	Járama	29/04/79	Scuderia Ferrari SpA SEFAC	Ferrari 312T4	*pit stop/tyres/Fastest lap*
7/*ret*	BELGIAN GP	Zolder	13/05/79	Scuderia Ferrari SpA SEFAC	Ferrari 312T4	*out of fuel/Fastest lap*
ret	MONACO GP	Monte Carlo	27/05/79	Scuderia Ferrari SpA SEFAC	Ferrari 312T4	*transmission*
2	FRENCH GP	Dijon	01/07/79	Scuderia Ferrari SpA SEFAC	Ferrari 312T4	
14/*ret*	BRITISH GP	Silverstone	14/07/79	Scuderia Ferrari SpA SEFAC	Ferrari 312T4	*fuel vaporisation*
8	GERMAN GP	Hockenheim	29/07/79	Scuderia Ferrari SpA SEFAC	Ferrari 312T4	*pit stop/wing/Fastest lap*
2	AUSTRIAN GP	Österreichring	12/08/79	Scuderia Ferrari SpA SEFAC	Ferrari 312T4	
ret	DUTCH GP	Zandvoort	26/08/79	Scuderia Ferrari SpA SEFAC	Ferrari 312T4	*tyre/suspension/Fastest lap*
2	ITALIAN GP	Monza	09/09/79	Scuderia Ferrari SpA SEFAC	Ferrari 312T4	
7	Gran Premio Dino Ferrari	Imola	16/09/79	Scuderia Ferrari SpA SEFAC	Ferrari 312T4	*Pole/Fastest lap*
2	CANADIAN GP	Montreal	30/09/79	Scuderia Ferrari SpA SEFAC	Ferrari 312T4	
1	US GP EAST	Watkins Glen	07/10/79	Scuderia Ferrari SpA SEFAC	Ferrari 312T4	

1980

ret	ARGENTINE GP	Buenos Aires	13/01/80	Scuderia Ferrari SpA SEFAC	Ferrari 312T5	*accident/suspension/steering*
16/*ret*	BRAZILIAN GP	Interlagos	27/01/80	Scuderia Ferrari SpA SEFAC	Ferrari 312T5	*jammed throttle*
ret	SOUTH AFRICAN GP	Kyalami	01/03/80	Scuderia Ferrari SpA SEFAC	Ferrari 312T5	*transmission*
ret	US GP WEST	Long Beach	30/03/80	Scuderia Ferrari SpA SEFAC	Ferrari 312T5	*driveshaft*
6	BELGIAN GP	Zolder	04/05/80	Scuderia Ferrari SpA SEFAC	Ferrari 312T5	
5	MONACO GP	Monte Carlo	18/05/80	Scuderia Ferrari SpA SEFAC	Ferrari 312T5	*pit stop/tyre*
8	FRENCH GP	Paul Ricard	29/06/80	Scuderia Ferrari SpA SEFAC	Ferrari 312T5	*pit stop/tyres*
ret	BRITISH GP	Brands Hatch	13/07/80	Scuderia Ferrari SpA SEFAC	Ferrari 312T5	*engine*
6	GERMAN GP	Hockenheim	10/08/80	Scuderia Ferrari SpA SEFAC	Ferrari 312T5	*pit stop/tyres*
8	AUSTRIAN GP	Österreichring	17/08/80	Scuderia Ferrari SpA SEFAC	Ferrari 312T5	*pit stop/tyres*
7	DUTCH GP	Zandvoort	31/08/80	Scuderia Ferrari SpA SEFAC	Ferrari 312T5	*pit stop/tyres*
ret	ITALIAN GP	Imola	14/09/80	Scuderia Ferrari SpA SEFAC	Ferrari 312T5	*accident/puncture*
5	CANADIAN GP	Montreal	28/09/80	Scuderia Ferrari SpA SEFAC	Ferrari 312T5	
ret	US GP EAST	Watkins Glen	05/10/80	Scuderia Ferrari SpA SEFAC	Ferrari 312T5	*hit chicane*

1981

ret	US GP WEST	Long Beach	15/03/81	Scuderia Ferrari SpA SEFAC	Ferrari 126CK	*driveshaft*
ret	BRAZILIAN GP	Rio	29/03/81	Scuderia Ferrari SpA SEFAC	Ferrari 126CK	*turbo*
ret	ARGENTINE GP	Buenos Aires	12/04/81	Scuderia Ferrari SpA SEFAC	Ferrari 126CK	*driveshaft*
7	SAN MARINO GP	Imola	03/05/81	Scuderia Ferrari SpA SEFAC	Ferrari 126CK	*pit stop/tyres/Fastest lap*
4	BELGIAN GP	Zolder	17/05/81	Scuderia Ferrari SpA SEFAC	Ferrari 126CK	
1	MONACO GP	Monte Carlo	31/05/81	Scuderia Ferrari SpA SEFAC	Ferrari 126CK	
1	SPANISH GP	Járama	21/06/81	Scuderia Ferrari SpA SEFAC	Ferrari 126CK	
ret	FRENCH GP	Dijon	05/07/81	Scuderia Ferrari SpA SEFAC	Ferrari 126CK	*electrics*
ret	BRITISH GP	Silverstone	18/07/81	Scuderia Ferrari SpA SEFAC	Ferrari 126CK	*spun off*
10	GERMAN GP	Hockenheim	02/08/81	Scuderia Ferrari SpA SEFAC	Ferrari 126CK	*pit stop/tyres*
ret	AUSTRIAN GP	Österreichring	16/08/81	Scuderia Ferrari SpA SEFAC	Ferrari 126CK	*accident*
ret	DUTCH GP	Zandvoort	30/08/81	Scuderia Ferrari SpA SEFAC	Ferrari 126CK	*accident/Giacomelli/Patrese*
ret	ITALIAN GP	Monza	13/09/81	Scuderia Ferrari SpA SEFAC	Ferrari 126CK	*turbo*
3	CANADIAN GP	Montreal	27/09/81	Scuderia Ferrari SpA SEFAC	Ferrari 126CK	
dsq	CAESAR'S PALACE GP	Las Vegas	17/10/81	Scuderia Ferrari SpA SEFAC	Ferrari 126CK	*wrong starting position*

1982

ret	SOUTH AFRICAN GP	Kyalami	23/01/82	Scuderia Ferrari SpA SEFAC	Ferrari 126C2	*turbo*
ret	BRAZILIAN GP	Rio	21/03/82	Scuderia Ferrari SpA SEFAC	Ferrari 126C2	*spun off*
dsq	US GP WEST	Long Beach	04/04/82	Scuderia Ferrari SpA SEFAC	Ferrari 126C2	*3rd on road/wing infringement*
2	SAN MARINO GP	Imola	25/04/82	Scuderia Ferrari SpA SEFAC	Ferrari 126C2	
dns	BELGIAN GP	Zolder	09/05/82	Scuderia Ferrari SpA SEFAC	Ferrari 126C2	*fatal practice accident*

Formula 1 World Championship positions/points

1978	9th	17
1979	2nd	53 (47)
1980	10th=	6
1981	7th	25
1982	15th=	6
		107

Formula 1 World Championship placings 1st – 6th + Pole + Fastest laps

1st	*2nd*	*3rd*	*4th*	*5th*	*6th*	*Pole*	*Fastest lap*
6	5	2	2	3	3	2	7

Note:

Gilles Villeneuve also raced snowmobiles for several years, winning various championships. He also tried his hand at drag racing and Canadian oval racing before turning to Formula Ford in 1973 when he won seven of the ten events he entered. In Formula Ford he used a chassis built by one Jean-Pierre St Jacques.